# Lost and Found
## The Lost Kingdom of Heaven

Gerald Hines

Copyright © 2023

All Rights Reserved

ISBN: 978-1-962464-56-7

# Dedication

First, I would like to dedicate this book to Jesus Christ. While I have never physically met Him, He has become my very best friend. He changed my life. He gave me forgiveness and hope, and He gave me the love of my life!

Ilosha and I met during some very tough times. Over time, we grew to be one in spirit and one in flesh. Jesus entered our marriage and blessed us in so many ways we were compelled to believe in His Power. Ilosha is my spirit and inspiration. She is also my sounding board without whom I cannot think, as I am a verbal thinker. Ilosha, thanks for listening to me over and over again as I wrote this book!

Lastly, I would like to dedicate this book to Aleliya, Charity and Jay, our three children. I trust this book will make a difference in your lives. It is my prayer that we will spend eternity in the Kingdom of Heaven together!

# Acknowledgment

I want to thank the rabbi, whose name I forget, for the sermon that inspired me to write this book. Seriously, if he had not been so arrogant to say Jews were and are saved just because they are Jews, I never would have written this. He went on to say that we Gentiles have a different path to our Creator, and when the apostle Paul said, "Both Jews and Gentiles are one in Jesus," that's not true.

Well, let's just say, I do not believe that!

I also want to acknowledge Blaise Pascal. His article titled, Pascal's Wager can be life changing, and I have added his "wager," with a few of my comments, in Chapter 25. Pascal is right in saying everyone should believe in God. He shows logically and statistically beyond doubt that everyone should believe in God!

Finally, many thanks to all the people in my life who were patient with me and helped me find my way to the *"lost Kingdom of Heaven"*.

# Contents

Dedication ................................................................. iii

Acknowledgment ......................................................... iv

About the Author ...................................................... viii

Preface .......................................................................... x

Chapter 1 ...................................................................... 1

Let's Be Clear from the Beginning: You Are Lost ........... 1

Chapter 2: Yep, You Are Lost, and You May Not Even Care! ............................................................................ 10

Chapter 3: Give Me the Blue Pill ...................................... 18

Chapter 4: Lucifer's (Satan's) Challenge ...................... 25

Chapter 5: Our Creator Wants No One Lost! ................. 32

Chapter 6: The Walking Dead! ........................................ 38

Chapter 7: Let's See - Everyone Starts Out Lost! ........ 47

Chapter 8: Why Do I Need to Be Found? ....................... 62

Chapter 9: But...I Don't Think I Am Lost ...................... 71

Chapter 10: If I Am Lost, Is Anyone Looking for Me? . 77

Chapter 11: Life, Death and the Second Death ............. 84

Chapter 12: Jesus Answers Satan's First Claim! .......... 90

Chapter 13: Jesus Answers Satan's Second Claim ....... 101

Chapter 14: Jesus Solves Challenge #3 with You! ....... 107

Father Is Sitting on the Porch Waiting for Us to Return ................................................................. 110

Chapter 15: More Lost Are Found! ............................... 113

Abraham Was 100 Years Old When He and Sarah Had Isaac .................................................................... 117

Chapter 16: Why Is There a Reconnection Fee? .......... 119

Nicodemus Had a Connection Condition ............... 121

We Must Die and Be Born Again to Enter the Kingdom of Heaven ................................................ 122

You Cannot Reconnect with God Yourself? ........... 124

Chapter 17: The Price of the Reconnection Fee .......... 127

So how do I reconnect to God? ............................... 127

And the rest, as we say, is history ........................... 130

Chapter 18: Choice - No Jesus, No Life! ....................... 133

Consciousness is not physical ................................. 134

Demographers Warn of Impending Population Collapse ................................................................... 136

If there is no Creator, then there is no right and wrong ....................................................................... 137

Without Jesus there is no value in life! .................. 139

Chapter 19: Jesus Always Was and Is and Will Be Eternal ................................................................................... 142

Chapter 20: Jesus said: "I am the Way" - (John 14:6) 155

Chapter 21: "Fear not, for behold, I bring you good news" – (Luke 2:10) ...................................................... 166

Chapter 22: I Had No Idea There Are so Many Lost People ............................................................................................ 176

Chapter 23: So What Do We Do Now? .......................... 188

Chapter 24: The Lost Kingdom of Heaven ................. 204

Chapter 25: Pascal's Wager ............................................. 218

Epilogue: Welcome to the Lost Kingdom of Heaven . 226

Appendices ............................................................................ 240

# About the Author

Gerald Wayne Hines likes to call himself a truth seeker. He is married to his wife, Ilosha. They live in the Dallas/Ft. Worth area in Texas. They have 3 adult children and 6 grandchildren. He could field an entire softball team if he wanted.

He started writing after he heard a very narrowminded rabbi explain to the world why Jews were favored by God more than other people. Jerry, as most people call him, is a very passionate person with a high degree of friendship with God, his creator.

Writing this book is Jerry's first attempt to explain his understanding of the lost Kingdom of Heaven. Since he started writing this book, he has learned just how many are interested in this subject.

Jerry and Ilosha love to travel and explore the beautiful places God has created in the world. It is on their list to travel to Israel this next year. He hopes to be able to meet some of his readers during his travels.

# Preface

Twenty years ago, I was exposed to a book called *Boundaries* by Drs. Cloud and Townsend. I was in a very unhappy marriage, my kids were messed up, and I was willing to try most anything to fix my life. The book showed me that I had a life without boundaries. It showed me I was trying the same things over and over while expecting a different outcome each time. Yes, that is insanity! And the pain of staying in the status quo was greater than whatever change may come. I decided to change and try some boundaries. So, change, here we come!

After *Boundaries*, God led me to study the field of science and creation. I learned that thoughts (consciousness) create reality, and from there, I began to study creation from the intelligent design vantage point. If we were created in the image of our Creator, then maybe there is more to my creation than just a big bang. My journey to my Creator and His "lost kingdom" had just begun. Now, I want to share with you my journey back to my Creator and His Kingdom of Heaven.

*I believe you will be amazed as to what you will find out on this journey.*

Let's start with me making a promise to God to write this book. He delivered on His word, and now, I will attempt to deliver on my word. My prayer is that you will listen to what I have to say, and I really mean listen. You probably will not, as most people think their life is just fine as it is. But I believe in miracles, because so many miracles have happened to me that I can't help but hope you will listen!

People do not know what they do not know until they know. And what they do not know is that they are disconnected from the source of life and are slowly dissolving back into the quantum soup we call death, never to live again.

Wow, what a way to start a book. But I promise you that I will not say things I do not believe and mean, and I certainly do believe everything I will say. Speaking of "belief," that is a very misunderstood word. Most of the time, what people call belief is "existentialism," judging truth by your own experience. Good luck with that. It will only lead you to a physical reality where you are your own god.

To believe, you need more evidence than just an experience. "Evidence?" you say. "I thought belief was just faith in something and/or someone without evidence."

It is, but God gives us evidence. He gives us more than just faith or belief that a light switch works because it just does. And for those of you who ask, "What if it does not work?" I respond to you that you still tried the switch because you hoped it worked. Question of faith: how many times have you seen the universe create itself by a big universal "fart"? None? I thought so.

However, on the other hand, how many times have you seen "the collapse of a wave function" turn energy into matter? None is probably the answer there as well, but that is because you may not know what it means to "collapse a wave function."

But I'm getting ahead of myself. There is plenty of evidence to support faith in our Creator, and it is my hope to show you some of that evidence, mingled with our Creator's words, in our journey back to the lost Kingdom of Heaven.

# Chapter 1
# Let's Be Clear from the Beginning: You Are Lost

You will hear me say this statement a lot in this book, in hopes you will understand there is a spiritual place to be found. The Bible says, *"And God looked upon the world and saw how degenerate, debased, and vicious it was, for all humanity had corrupted their way upon the earth and lost their true direction."*

**(Genesis 6:12, AMP)**

"Quoting the Bible so soon in your book?" you ask. Well, we all have our beliefs, and mine is in God's word. We all have our experiences. We all have our knowledge. I simply quote from the sources I believe in. You may or may not value the books I quote from, but the content is what I am focusing on. One example of content is my own quote, C/U = R. Certainty over uncertainty = reality.

Just ask the 9 other guys who played basketball with Michael Jordan. What happened with 10 seconds left in the game and the Bulls were down by 2? MJ says: "Give me the ball." Everyone was playing in Michael's reality.

I will give you many examples of quantum physics in my book, so if you need more than the Bible as a reference point, you will have it. If you are a seeker, you will have it. If you have already made up your mind that you are God and you know all things? Well, then just put the book down and go enjoy your life until it ends.

*Back to the saying that the world had lost its way. To where, you ask? To the Kingdom of Heaven.*

Yes, I am saying that you are probably lost. Furthermore, you are probably spiritually dead as well. *What! There you go making some bold and rude statements again!* You are right. These are some bold statements, but I don't want to be rude. I want to help you find your way. The first thing you may say to me is, "No, I am not lost. I know exactly where I am."

Really? And where exactly are you?

*The problem is you do not know what I mean when I say, you are lost!*

May I suggest your question should be what am I lost from? My answer is you are lost from the Kingdom of Heaven. Do you know what the Kingdom of Heaven is? Have you ever been in the Kingdom of Heaven? Do you know how to get there? Do you know what you will find when you get there? I didn't think so.

# LOST AND FOUND

So, I will begin by telling you about two kingdoms. Yes, there are two kingdoms or two worlds in our reality. The first world is the physical world we live in. A three-dimensional (I would argue even more dimensions) existence where we live, eat, breathe, work, fight, and love. We call this living. For now, I will agree. But our Creator's original intent for this world was much more than this. More on our Creator later.

The second world we hope to live in is the spiritual world, a world that is outside both time and space—a world of energy where no one is breathing, eating, or working. Yet it is a world that is more real than our physical world. This is the world you may be lost from and not even know it! On top of that, you do not even know how to find this world. Hmm, sounds like you could be lost to me.

I believe now is a good time to have a brief chat about the "collapse of a wave function."

"Ugh. What are you talking about?"

Let me explain. We know, as an observer, having a thought (a wave frequency) that syncs up in the field of undefined energy possibilities causes creation. That thought collapses on the field of energy possibilities to take shape in the material world. The collapse happens instantly when the thought wave syncs with the energy field. Matter appears. Instantly, it appears. No, it does not evolve, it just appears.

How does it appear? Your thought just moves energy from the unseen world to the seen world. Boom! "Now, you're talking," you say. "This is something I can see."

Well, it depends upon how pure your focused thought is. The more focused your thought, the more creative you are. Just because you cannot see your thoughts does not make them unreal. In fact, you cannot see thoughts at all. That is part of the miracle of collapsing a wave function!

Now we have uncovered a problem. Most people live by sight and not by thought! If you have read the Bible, you will recall the disciple Thomas when he said, "I will not believe that Jesus has risen from the dead until I put my finger in His side and in His hands." Later, Jesus told Thomas, "Blessed are the ones who live by faith and believe before they see!"

This is a very awesome comment that is missed by most people. For most people, seeing comes before faith! In our Creator's world, faith and thought come before creation, and then comes sight. Reality (sight) comes after your belief. "Good point," you say, but you want some more examples. Agreed, that is a fair request.

Let's look at some history. One story that comes to mind is when the children of Israel were stuck between the Red Sea and the armies of Egypt. If you know the story, the armies of Egypt were very angry with God and the Jews! I will tell you the backstory for those who may not know it.

# LOST AND FOUND

Things started some 400 years earlier than the incident. Jacob and his 12 sons lived in a different country, some distance from Egypt. Joseph was one of 12 brothers. His problem was that he was Jacob's favorite. On top of that, he had dreams that made him look like he was going to be in charge of his brothers. Not a good idea to share that, as it made his brothers very angry!

Jumping ahead in the story, the brothers took an opportunity to get rid of Joseph. They sold him to some traders going to Egypt. "Awesome," they said. "We have finally gotten rid of him! We will see what becomes of his dreams now." Remember, they were living by sight. Out of sight, out of mind. Whoever came up with that saying was mucho loco!

Okay, so Joseph went to Egypt, courtesy of being a slave to the traders. They sold him to a man who was one of Pharaoh's officials, the captain of the guard. This man liked Joseph and put him in charge of all his household. The problem was that the Army man's wife also liked Joseph. This was a recipe for disaster! Sure enough, the wife made a play for Joseph's attention, and he refused. She said, "I will make you pay." And she made him pay indeed!

Joseph went to prison. The man in charge of the prison liked Joseph too, and he put Joseph in charge of the prisoners. I see a pattern developing here, which we will talk about later in this book. Joseph helped some of the prisoners interpret their dreams. Things happened just as

Joseph said they would; one of the prisoners found favor with the Pharaoh, and the other lost his head.

Obviously, the one who lost his head forgot about Joseph, and the one who found favor with the Pharaoh also forgot about Joseph. Years passed, until one day, the Pharaoh had a dream!

Again, we will jump ahead in the story. Joseph ended up telling the Pharaoh about his dreams, and the Pharaoh made Joseph in charge of all of Egypt. Wow! This was a long way from his dreams as a kid, where his brothers were worshiping him.

Now, where Joseph's family lived, there was a very bad famine. As soon as Joseph learned his family needed help, he moved them to Egypt so he could take care of them. There were 70 of them in total. God was with Joseph and his family, just as his dreams predicted.

Four hundred years later, there were more than 2.5 million in Joseph's family! There was no need to teach them how to make babies! They called themselves Israelites after Joseph's father, Jacob. In fact, this is where the story gets interesting. The Pharaoh became afraid that these people would take over Egypt, and he tried to make slaves of them all. Nothing good ever comes from fear, as we will see with the Pharaoh.

Now, a sidebar. Henry Ford said, "It does not matter if you think you can or you think you can't. Either way, you are right." Thinking is creating. Hopefully, you have not forgotten that wave function thing we just talked about earlier.

Now, back to the Pharaoh and his fear. The Pharaoh was afraid, and he began thinking of all the ways that the children of Israel could take over Egypt. And before you knew it, he had created so many laws that the children of Israel were slaves of Egypt.

Now, there is another sidebar to consider. Whenever you, or anyone, try to control our Creator's creations, you end up making our Creator disappointed and angry.

After 400 years, our Creator sent a deliverer to Israel named Moses. The Pharaoh did not want to lose his slaves, so God sent Egypt ten major plagues to change his mind. The Pharaoh decided to tell the Israelites to leave Egypt. I would share more about the story, but I would never get my book finished.

The last of the plagues was God sending a death messenger to kill every first-born child of Egypt. How can you defend against that? Needless to say, you cannot!

Now, we are at the part in the story where we first started. The children of Israel left Egypt and went toward the Red Sea. Guess what? The Pharaoh changed his mind and wanted all "his" slaves back. Hence, he took his army and pursued the children of Israel. Eventually, they were stuck between the Red Sea and the Pharaoh's army. Not a good position to be in if you are living by sight!

---
*Living by sight takes no faith.*

---

Here is the point of this first chapter: our Creator wants us to understand that living by the God Spirit (one of the Trinity) and living by faith in our Creator God is the only way to really live. Living by sight is just living with limits.

Moses was the leader of the Israelites, and God told him to raise his arms and watch the sea split! From a sight point of view, this was a very stupid thing to do. But considering the option of just waiting for the Pharaoh and his army to come and kill them, Moses raised his hands.

Here is where the power of God begins. Moses made a choice, and God sent some wind, and the water divided! You must always choose first, before God acts. That is how God's quantum universe works. You choose, and then the wave function collapses, and the Red Sea splits!

Faith in our "unseen universal consciousness," our Holy Spirit, makes our seen world different. In fact, that choice makes our world a much better place than before. See, before Moses's choice, Egypt's army was going to attack them. After his choice, they were on the other side of the Red Sea, and the army had drowned.

It is easy to say "I believe" after the miracle creation event. But before the miracle, that is where most of you will say no to faith. Most of you will say, "If I cannot see it and especially feel it, I will NOT believe it." I hope this book will show you how arrogant and stupid a choice that is!

# Chapter 2
# Yep, You Are Lost, and You May Not Even Care!

For many years, I was proving creation by things like carbon dating. I don't know about you, but for me, dating carbon is not fun. Carbon does not kiss very well. Carbon does not carry a good conversion. In fact, carbon is very dirty. Make sure you do not wear white clothes, as you will get dirty!

Seriously, here is the flaw. You cannot use matter to prove creation! It does not work! Matter comes from energy and not the other way around. So, what is my point? Unless you understand creation, that is, the "collapsing of a wave function from possibilities," you will not be anything but a material physicist. You will focus on seeing and feeling before you will believe. And what is wrong with that, you ask? Nothing, except things appear from things that are not seen. Matter is created from "no thing". Life starts with Creation, and then you have matter, not the other way around.

Now, I would like to introduce you to Mr. Q. Who is Mr. Q, you ask? Can I meet him? Where does he live? Mr. Q (Quanta) has been around since before the beginning of time. Really, before time, space, or gravity. But the problem with Mr. Q is that he needs someone to decide (or observe) to help him make up his mind.

# LOST AND FOUND

Who is going to decide what Mr. Q creates? Who will collapse the wave function? Is there anyone out there, outside of time and space, that has consciousness and can decide what Mr. Q creates? Yes, and God said, *"Let there be Light."*

Now, let's go back in time. In the early 1900s, our world had a crisis in material physics. Yes, science thought that all known physical processes could be described via equations from Isaac Newton and James Clerk Maxwell. Isn't that a simple and perfect outlook? However, physicists such as Max Planck, Walther Nernst, and even Albert Einstein were discovering new phenomena, such as X-rays, the photoelectric effect, nuclear radiation, and these little things called electrons. These discoveries were causing a problem for the material physics community.

In 1911, from October 30 to November 3, eighteen of the world's most brilliant thought leaders in the world of science and physics went to a conference in Brussels. This was by invitation only and funded by the wealthy chemist Ernest Solvay. The guest list was very impressive.

This meeting caused one of the world's biggest arguments between 18 men. Maybe they should have invited one more. Maybe they should have invited the Creator of the universe. Maybe then we would have seen more answers to the questions from that meeting.

The problem was that some preferred classical physics and others preferred quantum mechanics. Einstein was in favor of some of the quantum mechanics discoveries. For example, he said light was both a wave and a particle. It took 9 years for them all to agree to call these particles of light photons! And it was in 1927 that quantum mechanics went off the rails and said everything was just a probability influenced by an observation. Einstein disagreed and said, "God does not play dice with the universe." Or does He?

Classical physics thought matter was the basis for life. In fact, science did a study that was called the Genome Project. It was a study to show that life came from genes. The goal was to prove that life comes from matter. That study did not end well for the scientists who wanted to prove that, and it was eventually stopped. Results? Life did NOT come from matter.

During this time, we were all searching for the origin of life in different ways. Some thought life came from electromagnetic waves. Others thought it came from photons or maybe from atoms or some kind of connection with energy and matter?

I am sure by now I have lost most of you. The quantum physics rabbit hole is one you will never return from. Sorry! I just want to say that our creator uses all of the sciences to create. He enjoys the creation of all life!

You may ask, what is your point? How does all this "science" relate to being lost? And what am I lost from again? And what does any of this have to do with me?

## LOST AND FOUND

To answer these questions, I will provide a short recap:

1. Consciousness (the observer) moves energy into matter
2. Faith in that consciousness is the power to create the desired result
3. Consciousness creates from outside time and space, from waves of possibility
4. You cannot create time and space from within time and space before time and space were created. More lost thinking!
5. All life came from a Creator's consciousness, His thoughts
6. "Have the mind of Christ," Paul says in Philippians, chapter 2
7. "Change your thoughts and change your life." -Dr. Bruce Lipton
8. You, yes, you came from your Creator's thoughts – Jeremiah 1:5 "Before I formed you in the womb I knew you"
9. You would not exist if your Creator(s) did not think you up!

Mr. Q (the science) has shown us that as we observe something, it changes by our observation or judgment, even when we observe it later in time and space. See the double-slit experiment. It showed that filming a photon of light being shot through a slit in iron and sending that recording to different people in different places and then observing that film at different times ACTUALLY changed the film. The power of observation!

Bottom line: there has to be a consciousness capable of measurement and judgment of an event that existed outside of our time and space reality to collapse the wave functions and turn energy into matter.

*"In the beginning God Created..."*

**(Genesis 1:1)**

The observer, our master Creator(s), measured the "void" and manifested our time/space reality.

*"By the word (thought) of the Lord (Creator) were the heavens made."*

**(Psalms 33:6)**

We can then say: *"Consciousness is the primacy of life,"* according to Dr. Amit Goswami. And God said it was good. Sounds like judgment to me.

Then, in walks material physics with the theory that consciousness equals mind, and mind is matter. And if mind equals consciousness, the consciousness must have been created. If that is so, then what or who triggered the collapse of the wave function and created mind? No one. But the wave function cannot collapse itself. It had to be that consciousness created mind. But how can something create itself before it exists?

Remember the eternal energy principal that energy cannot be created or destroyed? Then energy must contain a state of consciousness, a state of awareness outside of our time/space reality, an eternal and non-changing state of consciousness that can "think" and "collapse" energy into matter from outside of matter. Mr. Q proves that "Consciousness IS the primacy of life."

That is just what Mr. Q did in the early 1900s. Consciousness is the basis of all life. Consciousness is the creator of matter. Consciousness is the unseen God, the eternal source of energy for all life.

When I was chatting with Dr. Amit Goswami, one of the leading quantum physicists, I asked him if we could call this master consciousness God. His answer was profound!

He paused, and then he said, "Yes, you could call that consciousness God. But you need to understand that all conscious beings would then have to be created in the *image* of that 'God.'"

Hmm, let's see. In Genesis 1:26-27, God said let us make man in our *image*. Bam!

"Let's collapse a wave function and move some of those waves of possibility into the body of man, and then let's put some of OUR consciousness (spirit) into this body of man."

And Adam became a living soul!

*You were created in the image of your Creator!*

Now, as we understand the collapsing of a wave function, we begin to understand the creation process. Creation (the collapse) happens *outside of time/space!* This is most important.

Creation does NOT evolve. Evolution only happens AFTER the creation event exists inside of time/space. The act of creation happens outside of time and space, where the object is just waves of energy possibilities.

Adam became conscious the instant he was created. One moment, he was just a possibility without form and void, and the next moment, he was the physical and spiritual being we call Adam. This is the moment where life began for Adam.

Adam was created with connections, both physically and spiritually, to his Creator. This is the moment when thoughts, observations and choices begin. This is when I would say the "Oh sugar" moment begin. Adam began to create in his time and space reality by choosing options.

*Welcome, free choice, a.k.a. the power to create.*

Adam also realized that he had free choice. Free choice is the ability and power to create little sub-realities inside our Creator's reality. In the next chapter, we are going to review some of his choices and see what he created from those free choices he made. Spoiler alert! He made some very stupid choices. Some of those choices impacted the children of Israel we talked about in chapter one.

In Chapter 3, we will see what people do with free choice.

# Chapter 3
# Give Me the Blue Pill

*"Listen to Me, you stiff-hearted and you who have lost heart."*

(Isaiah 46:12)

I liked the movie *The Matrix*. In the movie, Neo has a choice to take the red pill or the blue pill. I love this moment of choice. All he has to do is choose! The choice will create his next reality! Remember when I said that as we observe, we create?

That is, by our choice, which contains a judgment from our observation, our reality is made. The challenge is, how do we live where the possibility is more real than what we physically create after our choices? The possibilities are endless. Reality is not.

We must learn to live so that the unseen world of possibilities is more real than the seen world.

I would like to jump ahead in the story of Adam and Eve. Yes, a woman is now in Adam's reality by God's choice. And God said that the woman was very good! At the beginning, Adam was very jazzed with Eve. Why would he not be happy? God created him and knew just what kind of woman would rock his world. Sidebar: Maybe we should ask our Creator to pick our partners? Food for thought.

So now we see that Adam is crazy about Eve. But Eve goes for a walk by herself. I am sure Adam was close, but he did not hear what happened next. Eve then sees a talking snake. Eve decides to have a conversation with a snake. Really? A talking snake? Come on, Eve, don't you think that a talking snake is a little weird?

Nevertheless, the snake convinces Eve to choose something that God had said would kill her. The snake took the fruit and, while holding the fruit, asked Eve if it looked dead. For Eve, her decision was, do I trust my sight in the seen world, or do I trust my Creator's words, who is not with me right now? And then the snake throws in the dealmaker. *"If you eat this fruit, you will become as wise as God!"*

*As wise as God!* she thought. Eve was tempted that God was holding something back from her, so she chose to live by sight. She heard a talking snake, saw some good-looking fruit that was in front of her, and perceived the idea (future state) of becoming as wise as God? Sugar! Yes, give me that blue pill now!

This was where she was living by sight and was deceived! First, she was deceived by believing a snake. Really? Then, she was deceived into thinking she would become as wise as her Creator by eating anything! How is that possible? The Creator created you. How stupid is it to think you can become as wise as your Creator by eating anything?

I just can't believe it. But we better believe it, because that is just what Eve did. And the rest, as we say, is history. Now I will show you that people have been choosing "living by sight" from the beginning of time. However, don't worry, I will get back to the children of Israel and their choices of living by sight and their blue pill very soon. Just permit me to finish my point about Adam and Eve.

What is my point about Eve choosing to live by sight? Eve believed the snake (actually, it was Lucifer talking through the snake) that eating some food would make her as wise as her Creator.

Let's stop right there. That is not possible! Food (matter) does not possess the power to change her wisdom. Food provides energy to the body. And food may dumb you down or make you sick, but my point is your sight and hearing can deceive you, just like it deceived the children of Israel in the wilderness, thinking that making an idol calf out of gold earrings would save them from hunger. Again, how dumb can you get?

You must choose to live by faith in the unseen world and in your unseen Creator. Why? Because your power and energy come from your Creator. But, but, but Eve said, *"the fruit looked so good!"*

Yeah, right. The senses will always make things look, smell and sound good, but that does not make it good for you.

*Consciousness, "our Creator," is the primacy of life!*

Eve then goes to Adam and says, *"You got to eat this food. It will make you as wise as God! I even feel smarter already!"*

Now, Adam has a different choice. He is not talking to a snake. He is talking to the woman who rocks his world. He recalls the words of their Creator. *"Don't eat of this tree or you will die."* Of course, they had not seen death before, so how bad can death be? Nothing bad had ever happened to them so far. Rather than saying to Eve, *"No, I am choosing our Creator's words and not your words,"* he takes and eats the food!

Adam is also as dumb as a rope! He is choosing his wife's words, who did NOT create him. He is choosing to live by sight and not by faith in his Creator. The woman was in front of him, and his Creator was not in front of him. His question of how bad death could be shows that he is living by sight and not faith. You and I know how bad death is. We know and experience the results of that choice every day.

Now, let us return to chapter one, with the example of the children of Israel. They had just received a major victory against Egypt, with the Red Sea drowning Egypt's entire army. And then, guess what? They started to live by sight. They started to complain again. It looked like they ran out of food! Really, they just walked on dry ground through the Red Sea, and they were worried about food? Yes, they were worried about food. They quickly went back to living by sight, just like most of us do every day.

This time, in the story of the children of Israel, we start to see an attribute about our Creator(s) that is amazing! Our Creator has a ton of patience. Yes, and I don't even understand why. He had just saved them from the Egyptians, and then He had manna (food) show up on the ground every day for six days each week and a double portion on the sixth day. And no food on the seventh day. Why?

Before I answer the why question, let me make this point. These people refused to live in the unseen world. They had no faith in what they could not see. If fact, even after being shown miracles, they still did not have faith in their Creator. My question is, how much do we need to see before we believe? Faith in the unseen is just too much to ask for. You need chemistry, feelings, excitement, from the physical world before you believe. My point is, faith must come before feelings and matter.

Now, if I was the Creator, I would just start over with a new bunch of people, but that is not what our Creator did. He has patience. Wow, does He have patience! Plus, don't forget to throw in that He has forgiveness as well. They kept complaining every time something went wrong, and they kept blaming their Creator every time something went wrong. They blamed anyone and anything but themselves and their choices. Sounds like Adam and Eve when they were talking to God. Adam blamed Eve, and Eve blamed the Snake.

By now, our Creator(s) had a lot of experience with being the problem for everyone's mistakes and misfortunes. We will learn more about His problem-solving ability for his children in the next chapter. He just keeps forgiving and fixing. And then more forgiving and fixing. And then more fixing and forgiving.

Yet people just keep refusing to live by faith in possibilities. They want only what they can see. For them, life is all about matter, all about living in a world where every observation is a judgment. Every judgment is a choice to live by sight.

But here is the major problem in living my sight: you get lost a lot of the time. Why? Because you can't see everything. Take the no food on the seventh day that I spoke about earlier.

A lot of people did not gather twice the manna on Friday, so they went out on the seventh day to collect food. To their surprise, there was NO food! How rude of the Creator. They could not believe that the food on the sixth day would keep fresh for 2 days.

However, God had a plan. He wanted to give them a day of rest! That was so they did not have to work on the seventh day. No work on the seventh day? A day off? Sounds great to me!

Yes, a day off! Nope, that was not how they looked at it. They were just blind. It is pretty hard to find your way when you cannot see. God was trying to give them a blessing, a day off, and they were upset. Today, we would love to have a day off to spend with our family and the family of our Creator(s). Or so our Creator(s) hoped.

These are just a few examples of how people don't see. Now that we see that they and we are blind, we are going to blame God again. And to our surprise, He will forgive and fix things again, and He will send us a Guide to show the way back to the now-lost Kingdom of Heaven, which Adam and Eve lost for us.

# Chapter 4
# Lucifer's (Satan's) Challenge

The beginning of rebellion. This is a strange mystery in the history of our Creator's world. Our Creator enjoys creating beautiful and talented beings. Our Creator loves beauty, symmetry, balance, and every imaginable design in nature and is unlimited in talents—so talented that they created one being that could sing all of the harmony parts at the same time! That must have been awesome to hear! Creation was full of all kinds of colors and light. This light was the covering of all creations. Everything was simply amazing and beautiful.

Lucifer was one of the Creator's beings. This being was the one who could sing all parts of the harmony at the same time, and he was put in charge of all the other beings (angels) in Heaven. He was very special. But he forgot who his Creator was and where all his talents and beauty came from. He became very proud of who he was and what he could do.

He was very powerful, full of reason and knowledge. His reason got the best of him, and he thought, *I am so awesome that I should be as important as God Himself. He made me so awesome that I can now become as powerful as God.* And he did not want to give worship to God the Word (soon to be Jesus). In fact, he did not want to worship God the Father anymore period!

Ellen White, a woman who saw Lucifer in some of her visions, said in her book, *The Story of Redemption*, "*His forehead was high and broad, showing a powerful intellect,*" and "*His bearing was noble and majestic.*" She also said that she saw, "*Lucifer was next in honor to Jesus, God's dear Son,*" and that "*Jesus (the word) was one with the Father before any of the angels were created.*"

The Creator assembled the heavenly host that He might clarify the Oneness of God the Father and God the Word (the Son) in the presence of all Creation. The Father made it known that it was ordained by Himself that God the Word, His Son, was equal with Himself, that He had always been and would always be one with the Father.

This would not have been necessary, except the Heavenly Angels that were created did not understand the Trinity of God. They all assumed Jesus had a beginning, just like they did. The best example I can use today is the Creator is represented by water.

Water can take different forms, including liquid water, frozen water, and steam. These forms are all the same water. But because Lucifer was the highest of the created beings, he thought that the Father would promote him to oneness with the Father. That did not happen, and Lucifer got jealous. You can't be "equal" to someone who was never made.

Quantum physics can help us understand why it was not possible for Lucifer to be made into someone who was never made. Something that is collapsed from consciousness cannot be equal to that consciousness. It is just not possible. An example is you cannot create a glass from within the glass when that glass does not exist. There is NO equal to consciousness! By nature, you cannot be equal to the consciousness that created you. When you understand that, you see how stupid it was for Lucifer to think he would be promoted to equality.

Lucifer, in his envy and jealousy, assumed that God the Word would rule with power and might and not love. He thought their freedom would be lost. Jealousy entered his thoughts and corrupted his mind. So, he told angels that henceforth, all the sweet liberty the angels had enjoyed was at an end. Jealousy caused him to lie. He reasoned, had not a new ruler been appointed over them, to whom they from now on must yield submissive honor?

Therefore, he devised a plan to become as important and powerful as God. Well, his plan was a bad idea and did not work. Jealousy is evil and causes you to imagine all kinds of evil.

Reason would tell you that if a Creator, without beginning, made you, then how could you, a created being, ever be as powerful as your Creator? Sounds stupid, right? Lucifer's plan was to get other created beings to agree with him that he was awesome, and Jesus was bad!

God the Son, Jesus, was no different than He was before, but Lucifer wanted to create doubt and division. Yes, at the base of every power grab is doubt! You must create doubt about who has power before you can take over power.

Satan made two claims about God, his Creator, in an attempt to create doubt.

**Doubt Claim #1 – Requiring accountability is not fair**

Lucifer claimed that no created being could live as God required. God said you must choose to stay connected with Him through His Son (The Word) or you will die! God had given them free will. Now, he said, that was being removed by God the Word.

God must allow us to be able to choose other beings to worship. And because we have free choice, it would not be fair to be required of us to worship Jesus or die. So, if free choice creates death, then free choice is not fair. God must allow us to worship any being we want to and still be given eternal life. We must be allowed to disconnect from the Source of Life and still remain alive.

In other words, God must transfer the Source of Life to within each of us. Let us follow choice. We know choice comes from possibilities. When choosing a specific option from unlimited possibilities, you collapse the wave function. Collapsing the wave function manifests reality. Choice moves energy into matter.

## LOST AND FOUND

*When matter arrives, it creates accountability.*

You cannot "un-choose" matter. You just must consume matter. So one may think they are not free to choose, but choice has a result. Lucifer said that God the Father must allow beings to "un-choose" and not have any consequences. This is how Lucifer tried to create doubt about the Creator. To make matters worse, Lucifer came up with a second claim.

**Doubt Claim #2 – If you make the choice to disconnect from your Creator, God the Word (We call Jesus), He will not forgive you!**

Remember, the **first** claim of Lucifer was that it was impossible for a created being to enjoy free will and stay connected to their newly appointed Creator, Jesus.

The **second** claim was just as much a challenge as the first one. He said that after one's choice NOT to worship God the Word and to separate from the Father, the Creator, both Father and Son would not forgive you! And if God would not forgive, then this new focus on God the Word would surely make their forgiveness impossible. And God would not let His disconnected Angels ever reconnect with Him. Again, Lucifer wanted beings to doubt the fairness and goodness of their Creator.

Quoting Ellen White once more, *"Angels that were loyal and true sought to reconcile this mighty, rebellious angel to the will of his Creator. They justified the act of God in conferring honor upon God the Word Christ, and with forcible reasoning, sought to convince Satan that no less honor was his now than before the Father had proclaimed the honor which he had conferred upon his Son (God the Word). They clearly set forth that Jesus was the Son of God, existing with him before the angels were created; and that He had ever stood at the right hand of God...They anxiously sought to move Satan to renounce his wicked design and yield submission to their Creator; ... Satan was stubborn...Satan refused to listen."*

God, in His wisdom, let Satan spread his lies to all beings in the Kingdom of Heaven. In time, there were a lot of beings he had convinced with his charm and logic. With wisdom and power, he said that his way was a better way.

Many living angels believed that "his way" was what was needed to live with freedom, life, liberty and the pursuit of happiness. Satan did not stop at just the angels in the Kingdom of Heaven; he went to the earth dwellers in the Garden and convinced 100% of them (Adam and Eve) that his lies were right. By now, he had so many followers that 1/3 of the spirit world and all of the beings on our Earth had chosen his way.

Lucifer's plan for the Kingdom of this World was to take over and destroy it. He conquered Adam and Eve, so now they were his slaves. He would set up his kingdom in this World, and he would become its ruler. That was over 6,000 years ago now, and we can clearly see what kind of ruler he is. Evil!

There is no Light in him anymore. But we will see how Jesus came into this evil world and defeated the two claims of Satan, and became the Savior of this World to those who believe.

An interesting fact was that our Creator did NOT remove our free will during this conflict. In fact, in His fairness, He put a barrier between Satan and all these earth dwellers so they could choose to return to Him. God, in His wisdom, saw that these two claims of Lucifer must be solved in the physical world. And in this physical world is where we first learn of the Man Jesus.

Our Creator made a physical body for Himself to dwell in. We know that physical form as Jesus the Begotten of God! I will spend the rest of this book showing all people that are interested in God's Plan how to reconnect to their Creator.

**Doubt Claim #3 – Unspoken challenge**

How was our Creator going to convince all the humans about His victory? How were humans going to believe Him? This unspoken challenge would turn out to be the most difficult of all challenges our Creator would face.

Humans would start from a lost and separated condition. They would be used to being their own gods and doing things their way. Most would not even want to look into the spiritual world and learn about eternal life. Most would believe that the one who dies with the most toys wins. I will show you through this book how patient our Creator is with us as He leads us back to the lost Kingdom of Heaven.

# Chapter 5
# Our Creator Wants No One Lost!

*I will set up shepherds...neither will any be lost*

(Jeremiah 23:4)

When I was a kid, I loved to play pin the tail on the donkey. It was so much fun to see where other kids put the tail. On the ear, on the knee, on the nose, and most everywhere except the correct location. A donkey with his tail pinned to his nose is a very funny sight. I realize some of you may have missed this simple pleasure, so I will tell you how to play the game.

You have a picture of a donkey, about 3 feet high and 4 feet wide. However, this donkey picture is missing its tail. Right there, you can see something is missing. Duh!

Then you have a separate tail that is supposed to be attached via a pin or Velcro to the donkey in the picture. Next, you need a blindfold that you put over the volunteer's eyes. The fun is that everyone has to volunteer.

You then put the blindfold over the person's eyes and give them the tail. Then you spin them around and around until they are just a little dizzy and then ask them to find the donkey and attach the tail to the donkey. Yes, blindfolded!

# LOST AND FOUND

The outcome is simple, good entertainment. What is my point?

This example reminds me of the children of Israel. They had been blindfolded for the past 400 years. They were not able to see God's work. They thought they were capable of seeing just fine. Really? They could not even see which way to go. God had to provide a cloud by day and a fiery cloud by night for them to follow. That is a blind group, if you ask me. They were placing the donkey tail everywhere but where a tail goes.

Now, if God's cloud was not enough, God also provided the children of Israel with a great leader, Moses. The children of Israel did not think so. They argued with Moses and did not follow the cloud God put in the sky. Why? Because they knew better. They thought they could see better.

Of course, they were blind, and God had to provide a number of examples to show them they could not see. Snakes, quails, the ground opening up and swallowing people, water from a rock, and so on.

The point is, people think that what is in front of them is what is the most real. Material physics must be more real than quantum physics because I see what I see. In their mind, both cannot exist at the same time. God consciousness cannot exist with a Ford Cobra. A Cobra is real (and fun to drive), and God consciousness is not. Living by sight is so much more fun. But just wait.

Lots of people today are just like the children of Israel. I heard a person saying to their companion that "the universe" was talking to me? How does the universe talk? We will explore that question in a future chapter.

People want to define their own reality. They don't need the Word (the cloud by day). They see just fine worshiping material physics (golden calf). Yes, they still have a "higher power" (not God or Jesus) by just talking to themselves. My reality is what I say it is. It is what I see.

That is saying I see more than anyone else. My vision and my experience are more real than anyone else's. Another way of saying this is, I am my own god! You are saying I am god, and my world is all about matter and my experiences. There is no spirit and no unseen world of quantum physics. No Creator. Just a few billion years of unobserved soup. Yes, reality is just what I make it. That means that someone who believes this way is saying they are their creator.

Now, our real Creator keeps sending guides (like Moses) to show us, His creation, the way back to Himself. But people keep saying things like, "I believe in a universal force and universal guide or some kind of spirit, but why must I believe in Jesus?" I will answer the question as to why Jesus is the Way in a later chapter.

Again, back to the children of Israel.

## LOST AND FOUND

They knew better than God. They continually forgot where they came from. They forgot because they were living by sight. I want what I want right now! And right now, the point is, the children of Israel spent 40 YEARS wandering around in the wilderness when the walking trip should have taken only 11 days. 11 DAYS! Do you hear me? 11 DAYS! How many days are you spending wandering around this world, lost?

We all must agree that this group of people were wandering around lost for more than 39 years! How was being their own god working out for them? Their choices at Mt. Sinai with an orgy and worshiping a golden calf were intelligent. Think about it! They melted down their gold jewelry and formed it into the image of a calf. Why? They lost their trust in Moses. They needed to feel good physically. They needed something that was familiar, something fake and powerless.

People have been doing this kind of stupidity for thousands of years. What is your golden calf? Who are you having sex with, just out of lust and physical attraction? They worshiped this golden calf and prayed to this calf and had sex in front of this golden calf, and the calf did nothing! Really, can you imagine a physical piece of gold talking, singing, blessing, creating or even moving? See, worshiping matter is stupid. Life does NOT come from gold. Life does not come from matter.

Life comes from consciousness! Consciousness is the primacy of life! Matter comes from the waves of potentiality via thoughts. Change your thoughts and change your life. If you say you don't believe in something, you limit your possibilities. Upon observation of the electron, the probabilities calculated by the wave function instantaneously convert to a 100% probability for the position in which the electron is detected and 0% everywhere else.

This is the collapse of the wave function. All the probabilities collapse down to one position. Life comes from the conscious observation of the probabilities. With God, all things are possible. Something (matter) comes from NO THING!

*With God, all things are possible.*

There I go again, down the rabbit hole of quantum physics. The reason I do is because there are so many people who think they know life. They are fine "doing it their way" from what they have seen, providing "self-love" because they are gods.

I am trying to educate people about quantum physics and God's Word and not just go off and tell people they are blind and dumb as a rope. Really, our Creator is trying to show us that we are lost, and we need to return to a conscious relationship with Him.

## LOST AND FOUND

Why do we need to have a relationship with our Creator? We could maybe understand why we were created. What is the purpose of our creation? What is our Creator like? What does our Creator want from us, if anything? Why does our Creator give us conscious choice?

The answers to this question and many more show us the meaning of life; they provide value to our lives and some answers as to what went wrong, why we went blind and are wandering in the wilderness of lust, passion, greed, fear and hatred. We need a guide to show us the way back to the Kingdom of Heaven our Creator made for us.

Where is our Moses for today? We can learn a lot from Moses, so we can see where we are going today. Moses was patient. He was kind. He was loving. He was **committed** to his relationship with God. He was a good leader. He was willing to give his life to help heal his people from their blindness.

In the next chapter, we will see what was stopping his people from being able to see.

# Chapter 6
# The Walking Dead!

- Luke 13:5

- Repent and change your mind or stay lost

- When you are not connected to the source of life, you're dead

God said, *"If you eat of the tree of knowledge of good and evil, you will die."* No, I won't, you say. See? I am touching and eating and doing just fine on my own. I am not dead, and God is a liar. Do you see this food? In fact, I have such a desire for that food. I can just feel that I am smarter now! Yes, I am wiser with just a few bites.

Well, that is what you tell yourself. The problem is in how you define wisdom or life, and because you were born in this condition, you don't even know what you—all of us—are lost.

First, you lost your clothes of light. The light that covered you is gone. Your clothes were so cool. You could change the color and/or style just by thinking. Sugar, you're naked and afraid! Yes, you lost your innocence. How much better and wiser you are now that you are naked and aware. What else did you lose? You lost your connection with your Creator. You lost living in the Spirit. You lost the fruits of the Spirit. But you say I am wiser now because I live by the sight.

Really, living without the Spirit is living dead. Be careful, you may see something that you will not like! By the way, what is the definition of being dead? Let us see what Webster's dictionary says: "no longer alive". Wow, that is profound.

Then what is the definition of alive? Webster again: "Having life, not dead."

See, material physics cannot define life and or death. Some would say that a person is alive if they have a heartbeat. Some say if they are breathing. And some will get even more complex. But none of these definitions speaks to a living soul, a conscious connection to their Creator. Life is consciousness and an awareness of connection with their Creator.

Then death is the absence of that: no Creator consciousness, no Creator connection. Yes, if you choose to disconnect your conscious connection from your Creator, you no longer have life. YOU ARE SPIRITUALLY DEAD. This gives a new meaning to the walking dead.

I think we are going down the quantum physics rabbit hole again. Your Creator chose and observed and spoke you from all the other people's possibilities, and you were created. You became alive because your Creator thought you into reality. Just you. Unique you. Pretty cool!

But wait, you say. I don't believe in a Creator. I came from a "big bang" that produced a tadpole and then a monkey, and then me. Of course, it took a few billion years to do that. But that evolution is not observable, so maybe it was a lizard and then a starfish and then a crow and then a cow? Yes, that must have been it. Really does not sound very scientific!

Your creator and you were connected by the Creator's Consciousness. And you were created in your Creator's image. That means you have the ability to observe. You have the ability to create. And we know that when you observe, you collapse a wave of possibility. That means in all your choices, you can choose life or death. But before you choose, please make sure you know all the possibilities. Please choose from unlimited possibilities. Why, then, would you choose to limit your choices and choose death?

*Empty the Hard Drive of Life?*

Again, why would you choose death? Yes, to separate your consciousness from your Creator. Not a very smart idea. Just ask Adam and Eve how choosing death went for them. They will tell you that being part of the walking dead is no fun. In fact, it is just plain stupid. Apart from your Creator, you cannot sustain any life. You are on your way back into the quantum soup of possibilities, never to be created in the same way again. And let's hope the Creator does not empty the trash on His hard drive of life.

# LOST AND FOUND

And then you go from the quantum soup's hard drive of life to nothing! You are apart from your Creator? You are disconnected from eternal energy and eternal consciousness, and therefore, your thought frequency no longer exists. You are dead-dead. Not even the walking dead. Just dead. Bye...

We lost our Creator connection. We are no longer connected to the Source of Life. Our body (a battery) will last only so long in this state and then lights out. The Bible calls this the second death.

Houston, we have a problem! How do we get reconnected? How do we come back to life? How do we live by the Spirit again? How do I undelete myself from the trash? I need an answer fast!

This is where it gets exciting. Just asking these questions tells me that we are getting close to getting our sight back. This is where we can find the way—Jesus. He says, "Through me you can do anything." Anything you say? Well, how do I get reconnected or reborn to life from death? How do I get the eternal life connection? Let's review the steps. The path is very simple:

1. Realize you are dead – disconnected
2. Realize you do not want to be disconnected - dead
3. Ask your Creator to forgive you for making such a stupid choice to disconnect. You are sorry for choosing to be your own god.
4. But wait! Why, I thought we were on the right path?

5. Yes, but here we find we are stuck!
   a. Why? Because there is a reconnection fee.
   b. "What?" you say. "A reconnection fee?" Yes!
   c. Who made up that fee?
   d. It is quite simple. You are dead, and what can dead people do?
   e. "A price for being raised from the dead?" you say. "That seems odd."
   f. But you cannot raise yourself from the dead, so someone else must.
   g. You cannot buy it, for you are dead, and dead people cannot pay for anything.
   h. Are you stuck dead?
   i. How smart was that choice to "do it your way" now?
   j. Really stupid.
6. Yes, but wait, there is an answer!
7. Your Creator has offered to pay your reconnection fee?
   a. Why? Because He Created you and He is the only one with any "skin in the game" that wants to rescue you.
8. But wait, there is another problem!

## LOST AND FOUND

- a. You are in a time/space reality and your Creator is…where?
- b. You need someone to pay the price in our time/space reality, where we are dead.
- c. Where the Living Dead are.
- d. And your creator is NOT in your time/space reality.
- e. Now what are we going to do?
- f. Nothing we can do because we are dead.

9. Your Creator comes to your rescue again!

   - a. He offered to take a physical form required in this time/space reality and give up His unseen God form.
   - b. He offered to collapse a wave function in the form of the man, **Jesus**.

10. Now Jesus—God the Word (in the form of a man)—can pay the redemption price in our world.

    - a. That redemption gift from your Creator in the physical form of Jesus is offering you a way back to the Kingdom of Heaven!
    - b. "Gift?" you ask. "What gift?"
    - c. Forgiveness and eternal Life
    - d. That is the reconnection fee gift!

  e. All you have to do is choose Jesus. Collapse that wave function and you are alive – reborn!

11. Now the choice is back to you, because Jesus is offering you a new choice.

  a. Do you want to stay dead?

  b. If so, enjoy your trip back into the quantum soup.

  c. If not, then go back to step 3.

  d. Ask your Creator to forgive you for making such a dumb choice.

  e. Accept the gift from your Creator that brings you back into connection with Him.

12. Remember, to be alive is to be in connection with your Creator.

  a. Welcome back to life!

  b. Good choice ☺

*This redemption path was planned from the beginning.*

  In fact, the plan existed even before the worlds were created. This is what you would expect from your Creator. The plan was to create us in connection with Him and with the power to disconnect if we so choose. The plan also included a path back from the dead if someone chose death—a plan to reconnect with our Creator. A great plan!

  Sadly, most of the people in our world say no. Hell, no! I want to stay doing my own thing. Give me the blue pill.

# LOST AND FOUND

This is a choice I do not understand. Even in the Matrix, I could not understand someone really choosing the blue pill, to climb back into the pod and be food to the Matrix.

Today, people are choosing to be "food" for the devil and his team. Today, there are companies and organizations that are created to protect animals from extinction. And in fact, we have a list of all the animals that are extinct. But wait! Where is the list of people who are extinct? Maybe we should make a list of people who are dying by their own choice.

The challenge comes when you ask the question, "How do we choose?" The how question requires that we know the facts. Where did you come from? What was it like where you came from? What caused you to leave in the first place? How did you end up where you are today? Are you happy with where you are today? If not, how can you find your way back? Do you know where back is?

If you don't know the answers to these questions, then how can you know your way back? Most of us do not know who we are and where we came from. We don't know who created us because we think we evolved from a "fart" in the universe. No family and no Creator. Therefore, what is there to go back to?

This topic is bigger than you think. Ancestry.com has spent millions tracking who our family is, but do they go all the way back to our Creator? Nope. Why? Because they would need togo all the way back to Adam and Eve. Sounds impossible.

*You belong to God's family.*

The man Jesus gives us the answer. God the Word is your Creator. You were made to be in the family of God. You are loved by God, and you belong to God's family. Without this knowledge, we have NO VALUE! We are just a result of evolution.

God says we have value! We have belonging. He wants us to come home. See how important it is to reconnect with our Creator and His Family. He is excited to drink lemonade (or tea) with us in the "cool of the evening". In His world, we are safe and loved.

Before Jesus went back to the Kingdom of Heaven, in the unseen world, He asked us to go out and tell everyone the good news about what He did. Through the man Jesus, the way back to the Kingdom of Heaven is now possible. The world has hope. Lust of the flesh, lust of the eyes, and the pride of life no longer controls the Kingdom of the Earth. All people have to do is choose Jesus' reconnection gift. We need to choose to have our names written in the Book of Life.

Which book is your name written in? The Book of Life (the family of God) or the Book of Death (the family of the extinct)? I have good news: there is more to the story. Jesus has made it even easier, as we will learn in the next chapter.

# Chapter 7
# Let's See – Everyone Starts Out Lost!

- Matt 18:13 – The shepherd lost one of his sheep.
  - The one that is lost is more important than the 99 sheep in the fold.
  - Why? Because the sheep is lost!
- Psalm 119:176
  - I (David) have gone astray like a lost sheep.

What does it mean to be lost? Does it mean I am physically lost, like on a mountain trail type lost? Or is it the kind of lost where I have lost my mind? Or is it where I just do not know where I am at all? Or perhaps I think I know where I am but do not realize I am lost.

Is your consciousness telling you that there must be more to being alive than just eating, breathing, getting old and dying?

*Is there something more to being alive than just my body functions?*

The type of "lost" our Creator is talking about is where a person has lost their connection to the Spirit of God. I am sure you have seen an extension cord that is lying in a box waiting for Christmas lights to be plugged into a power source. That cord is disconnected from its power source and does not even know it because it has no consciousness, no actual realization or awareness that without being plugged into the source of power, it has no purpose.

This is where most people live. They are not plugged into the connection state of the eternal power. Remember we talked about "the living dead"?

Now let us look at the 3 types of God's created people that are in the world. Yes, everyone fits into one of the three types. There are many ways to group people, depending upon what you are talking about, but there are only three types of people when it comes to God's children. We are not even going to address the types of beings that are not God's children. If you want to learn more about the children of the Nephilim, read Michael Hesier's book, *The Unseen World*. It changed my awareness of our worldview!

Here is the list of the types of people I am talking about:

1. People who live without the knowledge of possibilities. They have not learned they have any options. They are just lost and unaware.

    a. Therefore, they want the blue pill (matrix), if forced to choose. Otherwise, they don't want to even choose. Just leave me in my "pod" from the Matrix, and that will be my life. Sad.

2. People who live in the knowledge of possibilities and choose self-connection versus reconnection with their Creator. They are lost and choose their own way.

   a. They realize that they are not plugged into eternal power. They are like the extension cord that is NOT plugged in. They have no current value, and they believe they must figure out how to plug themselves into an energy source. They decide they are going to be their own power plant. And that is scary!

   b. Have you ever seen a plug that is lying on the floor pick itself up and plug itself into a power source that is 6 feet away?

   c. They refuse to believe that Jesus is the Way. They choose their own way to try to connect to power. Remember the song "I did it my way".

3. People that live in the knowledge of possibilities and choose Jesus. They are found.

   a. They became aware they were unconnected to the power source. They realized that this power was outside themselves. They choose to be reconnected to their Creator. They choose life— eternal life!

b. Their Creator, Jesus, came and picked them up and plugged them into the energy source via His Holy Spirit!

Now that I have identified these three types of people here on earth, let us take a deeper look into each type.

### Type 1 People: Choose the Blue Pill

These people believe we just showed up on this earth and they are left here on their own. No intelligent design. They believe life comes from matter! You can find a considerable large amount of information from the human genome project. It assumed that life comes from DNA, the 3.1 billion of human pairs. The base pair is the source of life itself! The underlying assumption was life comes from matter. No such discovery was found.

However, if you believe life comes from matter, then you choose evolution or self-creation. I am here because my cells choose me. Therefore, I believe at some level that I created myself. You have the elite right to pass judgment (observation) on all people, including yourself. Why? You are your own creator, god. You judge all things by your own experiences. This is existentialism. This can only create destruction and death because you cannot create life on your own.

People of this type are just lost and have no human possibility of being found! Why? Because they believe that they are *not* lost. They like being an extension cord that is plugged into just themselves. They call that self-love. They are trapped in what Excel calls a circular reference. They are stuck in a loop. That loop can never solve the answers to life. Welcome to frustration. Welcome to destruction. Welcome to death!

I have been talking about this visual of an extension cord that is plugged into itself! If you plug your computer into an extension cord that is not plugged into a power source, you will not charge your computer. You think you are charging until you turn your computer on and nothing happens. The computer is dead! It has no self power! It may be the biggest, fastest, most expensive computer money can buy, but it is still dead, lost from any real power connection. Dead!

Now for the good news for the lost people of type 1! How can there be any good news for lost people, you ask? Well, let us look at the word "lost". What does lost mean? It implies that at one time, they were NOT lost. At one time, these people were part of the family with our Creator. They were created special and in God's image, as someone connected to their Creator!

Lost means you lost your connection with your Creator. Thanks Adam! They are lost from the Kingdom of Heaven, the family of God. So, there is hope for them to be found. The question is, when?

If you were, at one time, part of God's family, then what caused you to be lost? Did someone make you lost, or did you somehow just wander off? Maybe some of your family made you lost. Yet somehow, you now find yourself lost. The path that you are on has led you to a different world—the kingdom of this earth, of separation, of lust, greed, of fear and of death. The path you are on is full of loss and disappointment. You just thought you had a real life. But somehow, things got messed up. Yes, you are lost and in need of help and direction.

Jesus offers that help. He offers His Holy Spirit. He offers the red pill. We just think that connection with our Creator is **no fun**. We think that God, our Creator, is asking us to choose a way that will cause us pain and be full of disappointments, a way where we must give up everything that is fun and enjoyable. What a misguided view that is! How can we think our Creator is creating us just to punish us and make our life miserable after He creates us?

Yes, another circular reference. We cannot trust God, and we cannot choose God because we think He is mean! Yes, we are lost and stuck in a loop of no trust or doubt, and then we self-medicate. Rinse and repeat. They do not believe God's word in Jeremiah 29:11. *"For I know the plans I have for you, declares our Creator, plans to prosper you and not to harm you, plans to give you hope and a future".*

That doubt loop can never solve the answers to life. Welcome to frustration. Welcome to destruction. Welcome to death! Sounds like someone is lost.

So much for type 1 people.

*Type 2 People: Don't want to choose, so choose themselves*

These people know that there are many possibilities other than their own way. They know there is a God bigger than themselves. Yes, there was and is intelligent design, and there must be something more out there. They know how stupid it sounds to say we just came from an explosion in the universe, and voila! Over the next few non-observable billions of years, life mysteriously evolved.

This theory is absurd. It is not even rational to anyone with even half a brain. Also, the double-slit experiment has shown us that something happens with an observation. A conscious being makes a judgment. See: **How the Quantum Eraser Rewrites the Past | Space Time | PBS Digital Studios.**

These people are just afraid to decide or to observe. Why? What if God requires them to give up all their earthly things? Or what if they need to change their decision as they understand more about choice? Yes, they are tempted to think that God is mean and wants them to be miserable in life. He wants to trick them into deciding before they know the truth. They forget the words of Jesus when He was speaking as to why He came. *"I came into the world so they could have life and have it more abundantly."*

(**John 10:10**)

I am reminded of my own life a few years ago before I was blessed by God with the woman of my dreams. I was always looking for a "better" woman. Yes, the woman I was with was good, but I was always comparing her to my perceived fantasy woman, my blue pill illusion.

Of course, this is stupid on so many levels. Let's just say that this belief kept me from ever finding happiness with any woman I was with until I was born again, until I was found! Until I joined the family of God in the Kingdom of Heaven.

The illusion that a better possibility is out there keeps you from creating a reality for the here and now. We do not believe *"all things are possible with God"*. If God can create the world or separate the Red Sea, then He can make anything possible. Yes, anything! You just have to surrender your will and believe.

The problem is, we live by sight. Trust what we see. We are the world of "show me". We think the day may come when God may let me down. We must solve our problems ourselves. we cannot trust God to take care of us.

Why is this a recipe for unhappiness? Because if you don't live by faith and trust that God loves you in the now, you will waste your entire existence looking for what never comes. Yes, that was me for many years, living for something that never comes, just like the Harry Chapin song, *"Cat's in the Cradle"*.

While in this life, it sounds like it is wise to "keep your options open," for you can always choose tomorrow. It really is just another deception. What you are not understanding is that there is a battle for your life. If you delay your choice, then you cannot find happiness now. Now is the great Superbowl of life!

The two teams are known as Good vs Evil. Good is the Creator's (hunters for the lost) side. Evil is the Killer's (consumers of the lost) side. Sound familiar? Life vs. death. Who is going to win in your life? Your choice.

Evil says that if you do things your way, then you have freedom and life. However, evil cannot produce life and happiness. Why? Life and happiness do not come from matter or any source other than our Creator. Evil can only produce the illusion of life.

Evil's goal is to make you think that life and happiness come from one of **three** choices. We will talk about type 3 people, but first, let us look at the 3 illusions to understand the outcomes of the type 2 people.

*3 Illusion Choices for the Type 2 people*

**Illusion Choice 1:** Lust of the flesh

This is the weakest of the three illusions. Desires of the flesh are very temporary.

- **Example 1**: I lust for rich foods. I then indulge in eating these foods. However, I overeat, and my body gets stuffed. I get fat and overweight. Here is a fact you may want to consider: in America, over 2/3 of all Americans are overweight. The outcome of lusting for food is overweight, lack of health, diabetes, and death.

- **Example 2**: I want to feed my body's sexual desires. I then indulge in having sex with as many people as I can. Why? Just because I want to. What is interesting is that when you make this choice and over-partake, you become stuffed in a different way. Merging your energy with someone else's energy causes a different kind of sickness. Quantum physics agrees with Jesus: by indulging in this lustful behavior you are only going to damage your own body. You blend your energy with someone else's, and you are marked for life.

I was reading Psychology Today a few years ago, and what I read was amazing. It showed that a wolf left its DNA mark on the ground, and the DNA mark lasted for more than 100 years. Yes, a footprint left a mark on the ground for more than 100 years. Imagine how much having sex with someone will leave its mark on you. It will outlast you in the physical world! Now multiply this by 40 or 50 or more sex partners. Then mix that with both genders. Then throw in some "other" sexual experiences, and you will become "the walking dead" very fast!

**Lust of the flesh** is just too dangerous. I will try illusion choice 2.

**Illusion Choice 2:** Lust of the eyes

- **Example 1**: Yes, this already seems a better choice. I will just desire to look at all the rich foods. I will feast my eyes. That will cause me to get a buzz but not get fat or overweight. Somehow, it seems to be missing something. What, you ask? My eyes are NEVER full. I just cannot get enough. It does provide me with some real satisfaction. When I want to just relax and have some peace, my eyes will hold me captive and demand more.

- **Example 2**: I will just look at porn. Yes, that will allow me to feast my eyes and adjust my energy myself, and it will hurt no one. Not even my wife or husband! I hear this all the time. Who am I hurting? I am just using porn for "self-love". Again, something is missing. My eyes are always demanding something more. I am becoming numb with porn, and I need more shock and awe to provide me with the buzz I was getting. I am never satisfied. I demand more to receive the same level of "self-love". I am held captive by the lust of the eyes!

Also, when we study what "self-love" does to a person's body, we will find that it just drains your life battery. You are built to share energy with your spouse.

Physical love is designed to entangle the two to become one flesh. That way, you build each other up.

The true definition of "self-love" is loving your spouse as your own body. In fact, porn will change your energy, and you will not want your spouse over time. Again, we find that the lust of the eyes still leads to emptiness and death.

Lust of the eyes is also too dangerous. Let's look at illusion choice 3.

**Illusion Choice 3:** Pride of life

- **Example**: I will just create an ego for myself! Yes, why did I not think of this sooner? Now all I have to do is feed my ego. I don't need lust of the flesh. I don't need lust of the eyes. I just need to feed my ego. Pride of life. I can even hide this from everyone else. It is just in my mind and my body. Wow, this gives me a buzz just thinking about it. But wait! Something is missing. I have no happiness. I have no peace. I can fix this. I will just create a bigger ego.

Remember the movie *Hook*? Peter Pan had lost his happy thoughts! Without his happy thoughts, he could not fly! Your ego demands you to be self-centered. It is impossible to be happy and self-centered at the same time. Happiness comes from giving love and belonging. Ego does not give, it takes. Jesus told of a rich man that had a big ego. He also had a lot of money, and all his barns were full of grain. So, ego demanded he build another barn so he could make room for more grain. He did, and he died that night. Too bad.

Pride of life is also too dangerous. Let's try a better way—Jesus.

There are many examples of these three illusions. All of them provide you with the illusion of life, liberty, and happiness. But science and spirituality both tell us that these three options for type 2 people are just three illusions. These illusions lead us to disappointment, slavery, and death!

Wait, I change my mind. What if I choose to believe in a Creator? What if I choose to believe that my Creator from the unseen realm really came in a physical form, and I call that specific form Jesus? Will I be happy then? Must I trust in Him before I can find out?

But what if I am wrong? Why must I call my Creator Jesus? Can't I just call him Mr. Universe or Mr. Wonderful? I like the name Mr. Buddha, how about I call my Creator Buddha?

### Why Must I Call My Creator Jesus?

This lost and found journey is a battle. It is not a physical battle. It is a spiritual battle. We will either choose Satan the illusionist or The Word God, our Creator. But, you say, do I really have to choose? I will just wait to choose. Maybe someone else will come along with a different choice that sounds better to me and my ego, and then I will choose! My ego (my pride) is serving me just fine for now. I want to live with limited possibilities for NOW.

This thought process can never solve the answers to life because you are delaying your choices. Choices are what you have in the now. No choice is effectively your choice. Again! Welcome to frustration. Welcome to emptiness. Welcome to death!

### Type 3 People: Choose Jesus!

Now that we have seen the 3 illusions of the type 2 people and their struggles, let us look at the type 3 people. They, like the type 2 people, have the same struggles with the "illusions" and temptations. However they not only know there is a Creator, they choose to submit to their Creator. They realize that we (people) were created by the Creator God to live here on this earth and be in a relationship with Him.

But this is where the path of life splits. The type 2's go one way, and the type 3's go the other. But when you are lost, you do not know which path in life to choose. Both choices in the path of life take faith. The snake (Satan) whispers, *"Go this way, and I will give you riches and pleasure."*

Jesus whispers, *"Follow me and go this way, and I will give you eternal life."*

The problem is, faith in whom? One way, you need to have faith in yourself and Lucifer, and the other way, you have faith in Jesus, your creator. So, make Jesus your choice.

## LOST AND FOUND

Jesus says choose me. *"I am the Way. Anyone who comes to me, I will receive them unto myself."*

Just choose Jesus. Satan is trying to confuse us all, as we saw in the 3 illusions. Satan still tries to convince me the Jesus choice is a choice with no freedom. But Jesus, by His life, has shown us all that Satan was and is wrong. He was a liar when he said there would be no freedom with Jesus! Freedom is giving up on our selfish choices, our ego, being our god and choosing Jesus. Be smart and be a type 3 person.

There are so many sci-fi movies that show people trying to find something in outer space to explain why we are here, to find another "path of life", to find value for themselves by creating something new. Or, as some of the elites are now trying, to find another earth to live on, as they believe we are destroying this world.

This world was just a random event, and we are just another random event that has now gone bad. This is a sad theory! They have no Creator, no Father that cares for them, no hope. They must depend upon themselves to save themselves. Some are now proposing to BLOCK out the sun to stop global warming. Maybe then we can survive? That is again stupid in so many ways. That is a hopeless situation. This choice ends in frustration, destruction, and death.

Fortunately, we have another choice. That choice gives us hope and a future! We will look in the next chapter at who comes to rescue us, who knows we are lost and want to be found.

# Chapter 8
# Why Do I Need to Be Found?

I am doing just fine! Being a slave to myself is not all that bad. Why does God keep telling me I am lost? Why can't God just let me live my life (death) the way I want? These questions come from a place of ego, a place where you are a slave and don't even know it, a place where you've been in the Matrix for a long time.

Are you comfortable being an energy source for the Matrix (the devil)? Being stuck in a pod? Being given a few visions in your slave life to keep you sedated? Just like Neo, we need to wake up and get out of our pod. Get out of our life of death.

Let's find out about our pod life by starting with a story from Jesus about the prodigal son. This son thought he wanted to leave home, that he would take the money (the life here in this world) he was "entitled" to and leave his father's home. *So far, so good*, he thought. He was tired of living under his dad's rules and doing what his dad wanted. He wanted a new and more exciting life. He wanted to do life his way! But life our own way has a lot of surprises—surprises that he did not plan for.

After he gets his money, he moves to a new country. There, he goes on a spending spree, and everybody seems to "love" him. Things are turning out just like he thought they would. Why had he waited so long to choose his way? But just wait, life without his Father has plenty of unwanted surprises. His money begins to run out. With no money, then no friends. Then with no money, no food. And when you spend money, you are not investing money. You are just spending money, and when there is no more money, then there is no more no more. I know. So profound.

It gets worse for the son. He chose a world controlled by lust, greed, and pride. He is in for all kinds of surprises. News flash: money does not care about you. People you have "invested" in do not care about you either. Everyone just wants a good time!

But wait, there is now a famine in the land or, I suppose, today, we would call it a recession. Guess what? He runs out of money and food. This is always what happens in a world controlled by stubborn, egocentric people. His "friends" leave him and go find someone else who has money to mooch off.

The moral of the story: in this life, you will suffer loss and disappointment. That is the core of this world. Fun, huh? This is where the illusion comes in. We think people are spiritual, but they are just living by the flesh. And we lie to ourselves and say this is normal. This is just part of my world we think. I should just expect this. Life is not that bad. Just a little setback.

But things get worse. Now what? Do I keep choosing life "my stubborn way"? Well, at least I can be happy knowing

I did not let someone else ruin my life. I ruined it all by myself! What a way to live. Or should I say, living dead?

When Jesus created us, He wanted something more than just a physical life for us. He made a garden for us to live in, and He wanted us to be in a relationship with Him, to share a family with Him, to go on walks in the "cool of the day" with Him—to be one with Him. He wanted us to have both a spiritual and physical life with Him. What a great desire He had for us.

Thanks to Adam, we all chose our own stubborn way. We choose to doubt God, to blame God, and to die. What an intelligent choice. But Jesus promises that *"whoever believes in Him has Eternal Life and will never die."*

(John 3:15)

We, like the prodigal son, say, "No, thanks, I want my own life and death!"

God, in His love, keeps pursuing us, and we keep saying, "NO, I want it my way." I have seen all kinds of excuses people give for not believing Jesus and repenting of their decisions and accepting His gift of forgiveness and eternal life. We say all these quotes that I am listing below and more. We, like Eve, want to be as wise as God and make our own choices. Here are some excuses I have heard in the past month from some of my friends and family.

*"I am too stressed out getting ready for the Christmas holiday to go to church."*

*"I suppose you want me to find one of those Jesus freak men to marry."*

*"I am just going to keep posting on a dating site because I know there is a chance it will work."*

*"I am doing this just for fun."*

*"I am bored with my husband, and besides, I no longer want him, and God wants me to be happy."*

*"I will submit to God, but you want me to honor my husband? Not happening."*

*"I mean, what does God know about what is good for me?"*

*"She is such a b**ch that I cannot stand to stay with her."*

*"She has gained so much weight (after the baby) that I just don't find her attractive anymore."*

*"There is no more chemistry."*

*"She is just too lazy, sitting around the house all day while I work."*

*"What's wrong with a one-night stand? It's not like I'm leaving her."*

These are just some of the lines we say to ourselves to justify our behavior. But what about our hearts? What about our promises? It is a good thing God's promises are not the same as ours.

So, the question of why I need to be found is simple. You will find an abundant and joyful life when you are found! And along with an abundant and joyful life, you will find contentment, peace, purpose, and family. You will find all the Fruits of the Spirit and, yes, the family of our Creator. You will find you are a son or daughter of your Creator King. The King of Kings is your dad! What a privilege. What an honor. What an opportunity. All it takes is for you to answer His call and let Jesus find you. And it is good for all of us that He never quits seeking us.

Back to the story of the prodigal son. Finally, he does realize that he is lost and decides to go home. He does, however, reason with himself about his return. He does not feel worthy to be a son of his father again. Sounds familiar, as many of us figure we are not worthy of being a son or daughter of our Creator either. But he figures that he would be just fine if he was a servant of his father.

He forgot who his Father was. To become his father's servant was not possible! But wait! He left his father to do this his way, and he reasoned that he must give up his sonship. He wanted to solve things his way. And now he is confused about his sonship. He was willing to become a servant!

A major point is, we restrict our positions and our worth in life by our action and behavior. You see, he was still his father's son. But now he is "worthy" only to be a servant. However, that is not how his Father sees him! He sees him as His son. We are just as valuable to our Creator after our stupid decisions because we are still His children. Yes, just because He made us. Our value is in our Creation and not our behavior. When we realize this fact, we can really rejoice!

As the story goes on, we see both sons did not realize that their value is in their family and not in their behavior. The lost son thought that he had DONE so many bad things that his father could not forgive him. And the "good" son, the one who stayed at home and despised the lost brother, needed to realize that his good behavior was not the issue either. The father did not judge either son! The father loved them both just because they were his sons. Love was, and is the key. Love does not judge. Love is full of mercy. If you come home, then you get mercy and a party (a wedding supper of the Lamb) with the Father.

*Our value is in our family connection.*

There are a few additional facts about the story that I want to point out. First, you don't have to leave your father's house to leave your father. All you have to do is judge and condemn someone to leave. Both sons were separated from their father. Both sons were lost. And for a long time, both did not want to be found.

What changed in the boys' lives? The wild son fell upon hard times. This is always guaranteed to happen in our physical world. Why? There is an energy shortage in our world. There is a spiritual battle for energy going on, and when you are disconnected from your Creator, you are fair game to be consumed.

Yep, I said consumed. In Peter, we are told that the devil is going around like a roaring lion, seeking whom he can devour. Why is he roaring? Why does he want to devour? When you study lions, you will find that roaring paralyzes their prey by fright. Their prey is much easier to catch.

Lions eat to live. The devil does not have eternal life and needs energy to stay alive. You cannot have eternal life apart from your Creator. How can you stay alive in the spiritual world when you are disconnected from your Creator? You must consume and devour other spiritual life forms to stay alive.

The point is you are fair game for Lucifer (the devil) and the other dying spirit beings. That means sooner or later, they are going to "roar" on your life. When the roaring starts to happen, you are on your way to death unless you resist. James says, "Resist the devil and he will flee from you." (James 2:7) Most do not want to resist. Most want to take the blue pill, jump back into the pod, and become a battery for the Matrix (devil). Just tell me lies and fantasies, and I am good. So sad.

# LOST AND FOUND

The first son's life path pretty much guaranteed his life would crash sooner or later. Yet, in some ways, he is going to find it easier to realize that he was lost and needed to be found. The other son thought he was still connected with his father. He thought he was favored by his father. He was not lost like his wild brother.

This viewpoint was what made him lost. He was judging his brother's behavior by his own behavior. Our Creator says that we are all lost and gone astray. We have all exercised our free will, and at one time or another, we choose to separate from our Creator and become our own gods.

This is where the first lie from the devil comes into play. He said free will means that sooner or later, you *can* choose to disconnect from your Creator and try things your own way. He said you would be "as Gods," knowing good from evil. And he said you would not be accountable for your decision. He said you could choose the "wild life" and not lose your Creator's energy connection. He said you would live forever without staying connected to God. That was just a lie.

That is why both sons became prey for the devil. Both were disconnected from their Creator, and both were fair game. There is another obvious fact I want to point out. When you are connected to your Creator, you CANNOT be devoured by the devil, you can only be tempted.

Your spirit energy and your soul are protected by God. That is where safety lies. That is where joy lies. That is where eternal life lies! That is why you WANT to be found and stay found! Welcome to the Kingdom of Heaven.

# Chapter 9
# But...I Don't Think I Am Lost

This comment makes me smile. Smile, you say. Yes, because of the stereotypical story that comes to mind of a husband and wife driving on a trip. The man says he knows where he is going, and the woman wants to follow the map. After about an hour of driving and not seeing any of the signs they were supposed to see, the woman says, "We are lost."

The immediate response from the man is, "No, we are not lost!"

"Sure," the woman says, "then why are we not seeing any of the signs we are supposed to see?"

They were lost.

Somewhere in your journey, you may have taken a wrong turn. How come no one told you that back there, you should have taken the "other turn"? In your spiritual world, there is something we call awareness. If you are not aware of the signs along the way of your spiritual journey, then you don't know if you are lost.

Where does awareness come from? Who is the voice of awareness (the woman, in our example) that keeps you up to date on where you are and what signs you need to be looking for? If life is a journey, then where are we going? Or is there even a destination at the end of our life's journey? We all need answers to these questions. Let us answer these questions from two parts of your being: your body and your spirit.

The first question is, where are we going? In other words, what is the meaning of life? The worldly answer is we are going nowhere. We are here just to enjoy life. Wow, that is so profound! The person with the most toys when they die, WINS. Yes, we came from a physical explosion of matter, and somehow, life just came from that explosion.

Life then took a few billion years (even though this explosion happened outside of time and space) to somehow develop a consciousness. Again, where did that consciousness come from? Quantum physics has shown us that consciousness was and is the Creator and NOT some explosion of matter. And here is the "drop the mic" realization: consciousness is eternal! Consciousness is spirit. Consciousness is God.

### *Consciousness is God!*

So, the answer, "nowhere", to the question of where we are going is just stupid. And if you are going nowhere, then how can you be lost? This is the worldly answer to the meaning of life. This lie is to please the ego and the body. I mean, after all, we live in this physical world, so we might as well enjoy life. Life has no value anyway because there is no Creator, just happenstance. Yes?

## LOST AND FOUND

Well, Jesus said, *"My kingdom is not of this world."* (**John 18:36**) Also, He said, *"Where I am going you cannot come."* (**John 13:36**) Then He promises, *"I go and prepare a place for you that where I am you can be also."* (**John 14:3**)

Question: do you know how to get to where Jesus went? I did not think so.

"I am the way," Jesus says in John 14:6. So that means if we do not know where Jesus is and how to find Jesus, we are lost. This seems to be a recurring theme. Yes, you are just lost and in need of being found. Jesus also said that when He leaves, He will be sending the Spirit to lead us into all truth, to show us the way. (John 14:15-31)

The way to where? The way to where He went. Where is Jesus? He exists outside of time and space in an eternal world—a world of love. We call that place the Kingdom of Heaven. The goal of our life should be then, is to find our way to this kingdom.

The kingdom of this earth is all about us. In this world, we exist to take, to consume. The saying is, "What have you done for me lately?"

Solomon set out to try fulfilling every earthly desire— desires of the flesh, desires of the eyes, and of course, the desires of his ego. After withholding nothing from his desires, in Ecclesiastes 1, he makes this statement: life is vanity, life is meaningless.

And yet we say upon hearing those words, "I want to see that for myself." How stupid the ego is. Even though Solomon, the wisest man to ever live, tells you that life is vanity, YOU think you know better! You think you are entitled to just a little pleasure.

If you do not know Jesus, you will always choose the desires of the body and the ego. Earthly (fleshly) man does not know God, and neither can the earthly man know God. The earthly man is disconnected from God, his Creator. Here is where "free will" comes back into the picture. Do you want to reconnect with your creator, or are you so in love with your ego that you are going to do life your way? Which, of course, you are free to choose. Well, you may think you are just choosing a better way of life, but you are really choosing death. Smart choice, don't you think?

Here is the rub. Your ego will never let you choose to reconnect with your Creator. Nope. You are a slave to your ego. Paul in Romans 8 says, *"What I do, I don't want to do, and what I don't want to do, that I do! Who is able to deliver me from my body of death?"* And he said this after he had met Jesus in a vision.

Now we see that humanity is lost and unable to find its way back to its Creator. As the song says, "We are on a highway to hell." Sounds like so much fun. Sadly, I was on the highway to hell for most of my life. And you know the worst part of the journey? I THOUGHT I was on the highway to Heaven!

## LOST AND FOUND

Again, never fear, Jesus is here. Jesus, our Creator, knows our condition. He knows that we are slaves to our ego. He knows that we will never choose eternal life on our own. He knows that we are completely living the lie that Lucifer told when he was in heaven, that we cannot live with "free will" and always choose Jesus. The lie was that sometimes, we just need to choose our own way. We reason, how big of a deal is that anyway? It's just a little bit of death. We call it a little bit of earthly pleasure. The fact is, you lost!

Let's get back to Jesus and His reconnection plan. He knew that we would all disconnect from God and be lost in our ego. His plan from "before the creation of the world" (Ephesians 1:4) was to solve the dilemma Himself. He would create Himself as a human, a baby human, and over His life, reconnect the entire world through himself, and in doing so, He would also show Lucifer that it is possible to live with "free will" and "always do the will of our Father". That is just what He did 2,000 years ago. Wow, what an act of sacrifice, of love!

Why would He do such a thing? Why would He come into this earthly world for anything? Why would He leave the Kingdom of Heaven and the spirit world of love and come to this death trap? You really have to be committed to your mission. You have to be committed to your creation. You have to be committed to us! It sure is a good thing it was up to Jesus and not us humans. We are all happy about that!

Remember, back at the beginning of this book, in Chapter 4, we saw the two challenges of Lucifer and the three problems that God needed to solve? So here you go, Jesus just solved problem #1. How? I will spell it out very clearly. Jesus, our Creator, left heaven and became a baby human via the power of the Holy Spirit of Consciousness.

Then, He lived in this death trap of a world for 33 years, always choosing to do His Father's will and staying connected to His Father by using His free will. He showed it was and is possible to choose God and always choose God. Then, He died and got the keys of hell, called the second death, which was required for the reconnection fee for all humanity.

By this act of miraculous love, He showed us the way to live in the earthly world and stay connected to the Father. He came and found us. Remember the story of the lost sheep? The shepherd (Jesus) left the 99 sheep (found sheep) and went looking for the lost sheep (that's us). And He did not stop until He found us. Now that we are FOUND in Jesus, what's next?

In the next chapter, we are going to learn what paying the reconnection fee is.

## Chapter 10
# If I Am Lost, Is Anyone Looking for Me?

*"In the beginning was the Word, and the Word was with God, and the Word was God. He was with God in the beginning. Through him all things were made; without him nothing was made that has been made. In him was life, and that life was the light of all mankind. The light shines in the darkness, and the darkness has not overcome it."*

(**John 1:1-5**)

*"The Word became flesh and made his dwelling among us. We have seen his glory, the glory of the one and only Son, who came from the Father, full of grace and truth."*

(**John 1:14**)

We now know that Jesus is our Creator, and His Spirit came to the earth looking for us. They had to come looking for us, as we were lost and not interested in being found. History itself shows this. Earth dwellers continually rejected any divine help. In fact, God had to restart the world once with the flood because it got so bad.

Jesus was, and is, our answer and the maker of the reconnection miracle (His life) and the payer of the reconnection fee (His death). To have a Creator who loves us so much that He has come into our world of time and space to live and then pay the fee is amazing. It must be very sad to have earth dwellers keep rejecting His love. But love will destroy all evil, you just wait and see.

Earlier, I said that our Creator had two challenges, and I showed you how He solved them both. After solving those two challenges, a third challenge showed up. This challenge was even more difficult than the first two. Why? Because He could not solve this one by Himself. He needed His family's help. So, He stayed on earth long enough after His resurrection to train some followers to be guides for us. That is beyond awesome!

His plan was to include getting help from His lost and found family. His plan included those of us that have reconnected, asking us to tell His lost family the good news of His reconnection, the answer to being lost. Specifically, His plan will show us how to communicate with people who live by sight and teach them how to live by faith. See, Adam and Eve choose to do things their way, to break their connection with God, to live by sight and not by faith, and to follow Lucifer.

Yet here is the rub on what happens when we try to help God. We think we are becoming more like God. We think we are making our lives better. That is what happens when we follow God with our own ego. We think sin is a better solution than following what God tells us. We do this all the time. We choose to follow some earthly plan, which is not God's plan, and then we justify our plan while saying, "I am helping God out." Moses was an example of this in Numbers 20:10-13.

Even after we think we are reconnected, we refuse to follow the Holy Spirit and live by faith in God's Plan. We only live by sight. We say we just can't live without sight. Now we have a crash! We need our Creator to come to our rescue again as we mess up His Plan to rescue us. God sent us Paul to explain how we are to live and to share God's plan with His lost children. We need to remember all the answers always come from Jesus.

*Let's review God's Plan*

God's rescue plan was to change His Form from God the Word and come in the form of Jesus, as we have already discussed. Wow, that must have been weird for our Creator to become created flesh. You would think when the earthly beings learned what He did, they would accept this form change for sure. Earth people seem to love all these sci-fi movies about the unseen worlds, but they refuse to accept our Creator in the form of Jesus.

Why do you think that is? It is because these earth dwellers know more than our Creator. That is because they think they are gods. They are proud, stubborn, and refuse to surrender all things to God. Again, pretty stupid if you ask me.

Now enters love, in the Form of Jesus, into our world. I told you that love would destroy all evil. Our Creator's plan included the Unseen God we call the Invisible Father, the Unseen Consciousness we call the Holy Spirit and the invisible God the Word that become the visible form in Jesus, that we now call the Son of God. You see, they are really One God with 3 different ways of looking at them. We call them the Trinity.

Their plan worked! All we need to do is choose their answer. Jesus!

Here is the outline of their plan:

- Create every being with "free will".

- If anyone with "free will" chooses ego, they will need a reconnection plan—**Jesus**

- The Jesus Plan is:

  o First, prove free will is a good thing

    - You can live with "free will" and stay connected to the Creator God

  o Next, the reconnection fee must be paid to provide a way back for His lost family

  o Then you need a way to tell the earth people that they are lost and they really should want to be found

- The physical Creator (Jesus) is the answer
- When we are found, we become part of His plan

This plan looks pretty simple when you outline the process. However, free-will people think they are gods and don't really need Jesus, which poses a problem, a very difficult problem, to say the least.

But not to fear, baby Jesus is here! What, a little baby? And born in a barn, no less? Are you sure there isn't a better answer? Well, at least no one can say Jesus had an advantage. Starting by being born in a barn and homeless for at least his first 5 years was a very difficult start! But God our Creator had a plan.

- Jesus started by living 30 years with free will
- Then 3½ years of training the trainers
- After that, He made the reconnection part (His body) and paid the reconnection fee (dying the second death)
- Then, He finished the plan through a 40-day advanced training class for His Disciples (guides)
- Then, He went back to the Kingdom of Heaven

What comes next is perplexing.

- The trainers (earthly guides) get killed off about as fast as they develop new ones

- Then, Satan and his staff persecute God's reconnected family
- Wow, this plan is suffering from tons of resistance
- Our Creator must see something we don't see
  ○ Jesus came to seek and save those that are lost. (Luke 19:10)
  ○ He saw the real battle was over the soul and not the body

There are two viewpoints from the time Jesus spent as a human that are obvious.

### *Viewpoint 1*

Jesus was not from this world. He said, *"My kingdom is not of this world...my kingdom is from another place."*

(John 18:36)

Hum, I wonder where He was talking about. Quantum physics tells us that consciousness is in the spiritual world of possibilities. Jesus was telling us that He was from the spiritual world outside of time and space, a world where love energy reigns supreme!

### *Viewpoint 2*

The second viewpoint is just as profound. This earthly life is not the end. There is more to life than this physical world. Yes, this world only contains the life and death of the body, but not the life and death of the soul.

There is a lot of confusion around this point. Most everyone looks at all life from their own point of view. Let's dig a little deeper and see what Jesus meant when "He said my kingdom is not of this world."

# Chapter 11
# Life, Death and the Second Death

I have told you there are two parts to the Kingdom of Heaven. Yes, that can be confusing for those of you who live by sight, but it is true that there are two parts. There is a spiritual part and a physical (new physical) part in the Kingdom of Heaven.

The Creator "formed Adam from the dust (body) and breathed into him His (Creators) Spirit and Adam became a living soul."

Yes, we have the body and mind (the command center of the body) and the spirit, together becoming a living soul. (See Genesis 2:7 and Mark 8:36.)

Many people believe that the body and the spirit are the same, and then they just throw in a soul, because soul is in the Bible. Now we know that is not true. Our Creator is saying that the body + the breath (Spirit) of God = Consciousness and life (i.e., soul).

What was Adam before our Creator breathed into his body? Dirt. Yes, just dirt. Ugh, not very pretty. Where did the breath (or Spirit) come from? Our Creator. Combine the two, and you have life, impossible for man to create as we do not have God's breath! Here is where things get very exciting.

# LOST AND FOUND

Our Creator says, *"Before you were formed in the womb, I knew you."*

(**Jeremiah 1:5**)

We have learned from our quantum physics scientists that "consciousness is the basis of life". Consciousness contains the thoughts of our Creator. Those thoughts connect with the waves of possibility and nature, then collapses the wave of possibility into matter. Now that is a powerful sentence!

So, the breath of our Creator contains conscious thoughts. Science calls those thoughts the epigenetic code, and those thoughts from the spirit of life that come from our Creator were *before* Adam and all people.

Let us recap. The body is full of water and dirt. The breath is full of spirit and consciousness. Together, we have life. Actually, two lives, or at least two parts. Remember, Jesus said, *"What does it profit for a man to save his life (physical body) and lose his soul (spiritual body)?"*

(**Mark 8:36**)

How can you save your life and lose your soul unless they can be separated. Sounds like "reverse creation," where the body goes to dust and the spirit goes back to God. Here is where we see that we have two parts: the earthly life and the spiritual life. Body = earthly life, and soul = spiritual life.

Wow, I am amazed. How did I not see this hidden gem of knowledge? Could that be because I had chosen to serve my ego? I thought I was my own god, and I did not need the knowledge that comes from my/our Creator. I was too busy just pleasing the body to even notice that I had a spirit, and that spirit was talking to me, saying that it was not happy. But I was too busy living to the desires of my flesh to listen. Sound familiar?

We first catch a glimpse of this knowledge of two parts to live when Jesus did not stop Herod from killing John the Baptist. After John was dead, Jesus said he was a great man in the present tense. (Matthew 11:11)

Herod had just killed the body but not the spirit of John, which returns to his Creator, who gave it to him. The Bible confirms this in Ecclesiastes 12:7 when it says: *"Then shall the dust return to the earth as it was: and the spirit shall return unto God who gave it."*

Here is where our understanding of the second death, or the death of the soul, comes from. Before we move on, let us look at some verses in the Bible that mention the second death.

There are more than 100 verses in the Bible on the second death! I recommend that you read them all. Many of these verses say that after your earthly body dies, then comes judgment. How does judgment matter if you are dead and gone?

# LOST AND FOUND

There are many references to a second death that speaks to your soul dying. This is the mother of all judgments! This is where our Creator judges whether we live with Him in the Kingdom of Heaven or He presses the "empty the trash" button on His Heavenly Supercomputer. This is the non-earthly death, the second death. The spiritual death. In other words, lights out! Our Creator "forgets" the epigenetic code of the lost souls.[1]

If when you physically die, it is not the final chapter of your existence, then what is the purpose of this physical life? Our purpose is to choose which path to follow. Earthly = Satan's path or Heavenly = Jesus' path. Now we are back to the question of who is lost and who is found.

Ask Adam and Eve what path they chose. They chose their own ego's path. With the free will that God gave them, they passed their choice of serving Satan on to all their offspring. Now, we are all born to follow Satan's path. The question, then, is do we still have free will? No. We are slaves to our ego (sin). (Romans 6:20.)

---

[1] https://www.openbible.info/topics/the_second_death

So now, we start from the position of being separated from our Creator. Thanks, Adam, I really appreciate that handicap!

But not to fear, for Jesus is here! We are not stuck as the walking dead waiting for the second death. We do have another choice. A choice to choose a Heavenly path, Jesus' path.

Here is the answer to the question, "Why do I need to believe in Jesus?"

Who has solved both of the "challenges" of Lucifer we talked about in an earlier chapter 4? The ego says, "I want the benefits of being connected to God without choosing God." We say that all the time. I really am my own god, but I want to fit in with the conversation. So, I will say there are many ways to reconnect with God.

"Jesus is a 'good' man, but really, Jesus is only one way to be found." That is a stupid saying. God changed His form to the man Jesus when He set out to solve the two challenges. Therefore, Jesus is God, and Jesus is Man! And, of course, it makes no sense to say I am connecting to God by NOT connecting to God. Jesus is the only way to reconnect.

The belief that says, "I can connect to God any way I want", is another deception of the original point of Lucifer. His point was that it is impossible to have free will and always choose God. Sometimes, I just want to choose my own way, the way I want to follow God. Pascal answered this question with some human logic and reason that puts to shame those who think they know better than God. See Pascal's Wager in chapter 25.

I hope you now see that having received the disconnected position from Adam, we are in a hopeless position of reconnecting with our Creator. The ego does not want you to find your way back to love and belonging in the Kingdom of Heaven. In short, Satan wants you to worship him. He wants you to think you have free choice and you are doing things "your way," but you are really worshiping Lucifer. Yes, there is no way we are going to choose Jesus by ourselves.

And don't forget that when you do it your way, you get to die twice! The earthly body death and the spiritual soul death. I pray that you see how dumb that choice would be. Pascal was right! Choose rationally where your choice improves your chances. Right now, your condition is death times two. I most certainly would want to improve your condition from death times two. You have everything to gain by choosing Jesus!

But now let us look in detail at how Jesus answers Lucifer's claims, outlined in Chapter 4.

# Chapter 12
# Jesus Answers Satan's First Claim!

*"The Son of Man has come to seek and to save that which was lost."*

(Luke 19:10)

This is where things get exciting! Our Creator, from outside of time and space, decides to come into time and space to find His Lost Family. He knew He could not find His lost children from outside time and space. So, He left the Kingdom of Heaven and came into our world. It makes perfect sense. If you want to find someone, you go to the last place you saw them.

So where did He last see us? Okay, we rejected the Kingdom of Heaven and chose the kingdom of this world. We chose to do things our way and lost the garden our Creator made for us. So, we must be somewhere in the time and space world. There are a lot of us, and our Creator wants to find us all. His plan to find us all must be a big plan, one that will cover our entire world.

But the Devil (our enemy) had his own plan. He must stop our Creator from finding us and changing our minds to follow Him. God's plan was so great that no one could stop

Him and His plan. It is a matter a time before everyone gets to make a choice. Then we get to live with Jesus for eternity.

But before we look at that awesome act, we must understand one thing about our world. There are two forces that exist: We know them as good and evil forces. This anomaly started when one of the created spiritual beings took the free will the Creator gave us and chose to create an ego. His ego chose to develop a belief of doing things his way, and the minute you choose your OWN way, you are no longer connected to the Creator and His life-giving power.

Now, the first claim of that spirit being was that the Creator was not fair. We are told his Heavenly name was Lucifer. Today we call him Satan. This being did not like that if you chose your own way and became separated from the Creator, you would pay the price and die. Pretty simple: unplug from the power source, and you shut down. He did not like that and wanted to live without consequences, i.e., free will and no accountability.

Requiring accountability according to the ego (or Satan) was not fair. He claimed that no created being could live as God asked. You see, living with free will demands that we must be able to choose. Choice collapses the wave function of possibility. Choice manifests reality. Choice creates accountability by collapsing a wave function into reality. Satan wanted to create doubt about the Creator. How does the Creator solve this challenge?

To make matters worse, Satan came up with a second claim.

Remember, the first claim and the challenge of Lucifer was that it was impossible for a created being to enjoy free will and stay connected to their Creator.

The second claim was just as much a challenge as the first one. After a choice to separate from the Creator, God could not forgive and let His disconnected and lost family reconnect. Why did Lucifer make that claim?

Paul tells us in Hebrews 4:6 that once you are in the presence of the Spiritual God and Father and you choose to separate, you cannot be forgiven. Something must be different outside of time and space! Yes, Satan was telling these lost children of God there was no way back to the Creator. No way to reconnect.

They had disconnected from Life's source and they were slowly dying. Their life batteries were draining fast. And guess who was sucking that life energy out of them? Yes, Satan himself. However, our loving Creator had a plan to reconnect all the disconnected families that had used free will to disconnect.

God saw that these two claims of Lucifer must be solved in the physical world. Separated people were not able to see spiritual answers. They all had lost spiritual eyesight. They now only had the ability to live by sight. In the physical world is where we first learn of the man Jesus. Our Creator (God the Word) made a physical body for Himself to dwell in. We know that physical form as Jesus the Begotten, born of God!

Then there arose a third and unspoken challenge for our Creator. How was He going to get people who are living in the physical world to accept His spiritual gift when people were so conditioned to living in the physical world by sight, that they refused to even consider that there may be a spiritual war?

Satan never thought things would get this far, so he never planned for what Jesus would do next. This would be the greatest challenge our Creator was going to solve. He would use His found children to help Him find His lost family. But we are getting ahead of ourselves again.

We get a good idea about Jesus in the first chapter of John 1. Let me quote: "In the beginning was the Word, and the Word was with God and the Word was God.... And the Word became flesh and dwelt among us."

That only left one question as to how the Word became flesh and entered time and space. The same Spirit of God that created Adam and Eve now "hovered over" planted a seed in Mary. Welcome, baby Jesus, the Creator of the universe.

You would think that upon the arrival of the man Jesus, the world would document His arrival and life. There are many facts that are supported by history. The first fact provided is by Time Magazine, with the quote, "He is the most influential person in all of history."

History was documented by specific historians: Thallos, Josephus and Tacitus, Talmud, and Mara bar Serapion.

There are at least 3 events in Jesus's life that most of history agrees on:

1. Jesus's birth

2. Jesus's baptism

3. Jesus's crucifixion

Also, the chronology of Jesus can be documented by non-biblical sources as well.[2]

While the man Jesus is the most talked-about and most influential person in the entirety of human history, a lot of Jesus' personal life remains private. I believe this is because His message and purpose was the primary reason for His life. He said, *"I came to seek and save those that are lost."*

---

[2] I have attached a link to: 30 historical facts about Jesus - https://testimon.io/blog/facts-about-jesus . I have also included this list in the appendices for your convenience.

Now, back to Jesus and how He solved the challenges of Satan.

Jesus' **first** challenge was to live with free will in disconnected humanity as a child and always use free will to stay connected with His Father, the source of all life. Remember, the first claim by Satan was that it was impossible for anyone to always choose love and not at least sometimes choose self. The problem that everyone found out sooner or later is that choosing your own way is choosing death.

Lucifer found that out too. He began to lose energy and started to die. So, what do you think he did? Yes, he learned to take the remaining energy from the disconnected lost children of God and consume their life energy for himself. (See 1 Peter 5:8)

We have made some movies about this, like *Highlander*, whereupon the beheading of a person, the one that did the killing, received all the remaining power of the dead person.

Now back to Jesus. By the time Jesus was 30, he had proven that living with free will in a physical body that was conditioned by separation was possible. In fact, Jesus confirmed this challenge by passing 3 major tests.

*Life Test #1*

The **first test** was to use His power to turn stones into bread. (Matthew 4:1-4) This was just a simple temptation for Jesus to use His power to take care of his physical body's needs.

When tempted by Satan, please notice Jesus' answer to his suggestion (temptation). He quoted the Word of God: *"It is written Man shall not live on bread alone, but on every word that comes from the mouth of God."*

(**Matthew 4:4**)

His point is that the physical body is sustained and kept alive by God's **words**. Wow, you mean the love connection with the Father keeps the physical body alive. From an ego viewpoint, that was impossible. A small mistake of Lucifer.

To a person living in our physical world, going without food for 40 days is not smart. Here is where all kinds of diets come on the scene. Fast for 40 days? Not happening. We will do a juice diet, and vegetable diet, a meat or protein diet. We would find some way to live without going without any food. But that is what Jesus did. Forty days and no food! He was taking His body to the physical limits to show that the body survives on God's Word and not food alone. Jesus defeated the lust of the flesh.

*Score: Jesus 1; Lucifer 0*

*Life Test #2*

Okay, never mind then, Jesus, Satan will try something different. He reasoned that if, after 40 days with no food,

Jesus chose to stay connected to His Father's Word, then Satan would try a different approach. He would test Jesus to see if He really believed that He was connected to His Father. (Matthew 4:5-7)

Satan thought this was a great idea. If Jesus is still hungry and claiming to be connected to His Father's Word, then encourage Jesus to prove it. Make Jesus doubt, if possible. Doubt comes from trusting what you see vs. trusting what you believe.

*"If you are the Son of God, then jump off the roof of the temple and prove it."* This is very similar to his temptation to Eve, where he quoted just part of the word of God to create doubt in Eve.

Now, Satan decides to quote just part of the Word of God. If Jesus' answer to Satan's first suggestion (temptation) was to quote the Word of God, Satan decided his response would be to quote the Word of God as well.

He quoted, *"He (God) will command his angels concerning you, and they will lift you up in their hands, so that you will not strike your foot against a stone."*

(**Psalms 91:11-12**)

*I've got him now*, Satan thought. He was using God's own Words to tempt Jesus to doubt. *Let me see how Jesus deals with this one.*

*Knowing God's Word is the only way to keep from doubting*

Jesus was well grounded in His Father's Word. He knew the difference between presumption and trust. Once again, notice Jesus' answer. *"It is also written: 'Do not put the Lord your God to the test.'"*

**(Deuteronomy 6:16)**

Now we see the battle of the Word of God against the Word of God. Presumption vs. trust. Ego vs. love. Doubt vs. faith. Now Satan is pissed. He is being schooled at his own game. **Truth does not come from doubt.** Notice the word *"if"* you are the Son of God did not work with Jesus.

*Score: Jesus 2; Lucifer 0*

What Satan does next is not surprising. He reveals his true colors. What does ego want most of all? He wants to be the center of attention, "to be like the Most High." (Isaiah 14:14)

Yes, it is all about me, he says. This is the basis of ego. This can never work, as he is not the source of life. Why? Because the source of life is love, which means it is more blessed to give than to receive. But ego wanted to make it all about ME! To get Jesus' attention and worship.

*Life Test #3*

Okay, so what was the temptation going to be now? Satan was not trying to deceive anymore. This time, he used greed and fear as the temptation: to appeal to the **pride of life**. We learned that greed and fear was, and is, the strongest temptation if you are separated from God's love, but it is a very stupid temptation if you are connected to God's love.

You see, ego cannot see from a different point of view other than its own. So, here goes: "and Satan took Jesus to a very high mountain and showed Him all the kingdoms of the world and their splendor." Sounds like an illusion to me. And, of course, love really wants what other people have. Right?

Of course not! How can the kingdom of this world be a temptation to the Creator of the Kingdom of Heaven and all things?

Satan goes on: *"All this I will give you if you will bow down and worship me."* (See Matthew 4:8-11)

Really, Satan, you made all this splendor? I am reminded that all that glitters is not gold. Is this world really yours to give? The problem with this "promise" from Satan is that it is a lie. Yes, one small detail. Jesus was, and is, the Creator of this World. He would have to disconnect with His Father and His Word to be able to worship Satan, and for what? An illusion.

This is always what Satan does. He promises you something he can never deliver. Why? Because he does not own what he does not have. Today, we call that overpromising and underdelivering.

Jesus' final answer to Satan is: *"Away from me for it is written: 'Worship the lord your God, and serve him only!'"* (See Deuteronomy 6:13 and James 4:7)

Final answer? **Yes, final answer**. And that means final answer! Game over, Lucifer. Jesus's connection is intact. Greed and fear took no captives. If the victim (Jesus) is too much work and it takes more energy than it will yield up, Satan moves on to consume a new energy source. The result of temptation #3 is: "And Satan left Him."

*Score: Jesus 3; Lucifer 0*

Notice the result when Jesus resisted temptation. "And the angels came and attended Him." (Matthew 4:11)

When he resisted disconnecting from His Father using His free will, then the Father sent Angels to strengthen him. Always expect the unexpected when it comes to love.

If you think claim 1 and the 3 tests Jesus passed were exciting, wait until chapter 13, where we see how Jesus reconnects to His children in solving claim 2.

# Chapter 13
# Jesus Answers Satan's Second Claim

*"Jesus abolished in His flesh the law of Commandments and decrees. He did this to create in Himself one new man out of the two, thus making peace. And reconciling both of them (the disconnected) to God in His body through the cross, by which He reconnected all people, so making One New Living Being."*

**(Ephesians 2:16)**

That is a loaded text, you might say. I agree. There is a lot to unpack in this text. First, let us recap just a little of the first claim from the last chapter.

**Challenge | Claim 1**: Jesus had to prove it was possible to live in this time and space reality in a physical body with 'free will' and still have the choice to stay connected to His Creator. Jesus met and solved that challenge with His Life. Living with Free Choice and always choosing our Creator is a done deal!

Now for **Claim 2**.

**Challenge | Claim 2**: God will not forgive His Children and let His Children reconnect with Him. How could Jesus reconnect to all of His creation at the same time? This task may be a little more difficult than God thought. Why, you say? Because most of God's creations choose separation from their Creator. Most don't want to be found or forgiven. Most want to be left alone and take the 'Blue Pill.'

As a result, we begin to die, like any disconnected being does. We must finish dying before we can be reconnected. But how can we be reborn without being connected to the Life Source? You see, when you use your 'free will' to disconnect, then you damage the point of connection. Jesus must figure that out for us. Never fear; Jesus is here! He would have to pay the 'reconnection fee' (dying the Spiritual or second death) to give us the power to choose to be reborn.

That reconnection point needs some restoration work to make the reconnection possible. That reconnection point is a spiritual reconnection for the reconnection to be complete. The result of disconnection from the source of life is death (spiritual death plus physical death).

With none of life's energy flowing through you, you get an immediate spiritual death and a slow physical death. Like Adam, Jesus had to take the entire Family of God in Himself to become the second Adam. He needed to secure the reconnect part by taking the entire human race in Himself. This human part was located in Hell. He had to suffer the second death to take humanity to hell and back to pay for the reconnection fee. What is the second death, you ask? How can you die twice? Well, it appears that you can.

# LOST AND FOUND

## *Get out of the Trash of the hard drive of Life!*

Your first death is the result of the choice of free will to follow Satan and become your own god. This is an immediate Spiritual Death and a disconnection from the Energy Life Source. We call this a slow physical death., i.e., you get old and die.

Now, if that is not enough, there is a ***complete death***. You (that morphogenic code) are still on the hard drive of life but in the trash. That is to say, you are in 'soul sleep.' But as you know, the trash folder of the hard drive of life must still be emptied or restored. In other words, you either get deleted or restored from the hard drive of life. One day, God will empty the heavenly hard drive, and your name will be deleted, or you will repent and *get out of the trash*. How do you get restored from the heavenly hard drive's trash? A very good question to know the answer to!

Most of us have a computer and have put a file in the trash. That is like your choice of following Satan: life in the trash. However, if you no longer need that file on your hard disk, you just empty the trash! That results in permanent removal from the hard drive.

The second death is just that; permanent removal from God's universe. To suffer that experience is like the saying, "That's all, folks." However, upon accepting Jesus' second death payment for the reconnection fee, you become spiritually alive (born again). To accept Jesus' Spiritual

Death as the required part of reconnection, we are forgiven. Our 'free will' choice to disconnect and follow Satan is reversed. We are restored back to our place in God's Heavenly Hard Drive. This is good news!

Your choice today is forgiveness and reconnection or permanent removal from God's universe! Not a very hard decision to make for sure. But how did Jesus pay this price, you ask? This was the experience He suffered on the cross and the three days He spent physically in the tomb and spiritually in hell, getting the keys of death for humanity!

Remember when Jesus said on the cross, "My Father, my Father, why have you forsaken Me?" This started the weekend experience of the second death. That is one experience I do not ever want to experience! But that is not where life needs to end. Accepting Jesus' weekend in hell can mark the new beginning of life for those that accept the price Jesus paid for the reconnection.

I recap; you were born disconnected from God, your creator, thanks to Adam. Just like every other decision, there is some result that happens. When you choose to buy a car, you do get a car. However, you also get a loan that requires payments or a price that you must pay the seller at the time of purchase. Either way, you must exchange something to get the car. Cause and effect. Isn't that just terrible? The car was *not* free!

However, Jesus offers His second death sacrifice and payment for you for free. All you have to do is choose with your free will, repent for your bad choices, and accept His Free Gift.

Now, you are following Jesus instead of Satan. Free Gift, you say? Yes, I say. How come people don't choose Jesus instead of Satan all the time? It seems to me that choosing Jesus is the only smart choice. Satan only offers a physical death and Soul Sleep and then, for good measure, the spiritual second death that he forgot to mention— permanent removal from God's universe.

*People think there is no real life outside of time and space– there IS!*

Yes, people are stupid! They think that a few days in this spacetime world is all there is for life. They think there is no life outside of time and space. This is a very 'fuzzy navel' viewpoint; if I cannot see or measure it, it does not exist. This is wrong in so many ways. Again, this is existentialism, i.e., measuring truth by your own experience. This is like a little child covering their eyes and thinking that no one can see them.

As we study the second death and its impact on people, we are learning the meaning of life. This is back to the point that people are lost and don't even know. Lost how? Not knowing that choosing Satan will result in your permanent removal from life itself, you don't know what you don't know. You don't know you are lost from the source of life and on a highway to hell. And our Creator is just delaying as long as possible before the "trash" will need to be emptied. And that is seriously some bad news.

I believe we want a different outcome, an eternal life, a life outside of time and space, a life that has no Greed and Fear, a life full of Love, Joy, and Peace. I believe we all want to live where eternal love controls everything—a place where love destroys darkness and evil.

So, let us get back to understanding how we can be found, how we can reconnect with our creator, and find eternal life. But wait, our Creator is already out looking for us, His lost creation!

# Chapter 14
# Jesus Solves Challenge #3 with You!

*"But it was fitting to celebrate and be glad, because this brother of yours was dead and is alive again; he was lost and is found."*

**(Luke 15:32)**

More from the story of the Lost Son from Chapter 8. There are so many gems of knowledge hidden in this story and I can't wait to share. So, I will tell you the outline and ending first!

- The youngest son was serving Satan. "I want my share of the estate and I want it now," he said.
- The son spent his entire value of his estate on "wild living"
- Life turned on the younger son, as life always does when you live just for yourself. And guess what? He ended up feeding pigs!
- Can you imagine the son gets some wisdom from feeding pigs
- The son goes back to his father to be just a servant

- But the father is doing something that he does not expect
- The father is sitting on the porch waiting and watching for the return of the son
- The father goes out to meet the son
- The father forgives the son before the son can say a word
- The father celebrates the son's return
- The older son is upset and does not want to forgive his brother but wants to judge him
- The father then reasons with the older son and shows that forgiveness and reconnection is the goal of the father.
- The father provides reconnection and forgiveness for both sons
- PS: the older son does inherit all the estate that the father has!

Now, let us unpack the story. There are 2 sons. At first, we think there is one good son and one bad son, but as we will see, there are only bad sons. The oblivious bad son is the one that we all see is living in the physical world to serve the lusts of the flesh and the desires of the ego.

I want to ask the question, if you are serving Satan, isn't this behavior just natural? Serving your lusts of the flesh, lusts of the eyes and the pride of life seems the natural way to live. The younger and bad son was just living in the physical earthly world.

Here is where the first hidden gem in Jesus's story shows up. Earthly dwellers, who are not connected with their Creator will always be takers! They will act friendly, but they are just "giving to take". I am sure you know some of those types of people. Maybe you are one of them?

The bad son loves the attention (feeding his ego), and he just keeps spending his father's money. Then, when his money runs out, so do his "friends". I am sure you have experienced the loss of friends when you run into hard times.

However, the bad son did have some survival skills. He was smart enough to at least try to get a job. He took the only job he could find, and it was feeding pigs. See, there was a famine (hard times) in the land, and there was not much work to be found. However, feeding pigs was not much fun for a person living for their fleshly desires and pride in life. So, he began to think.

Our next gem is our Creator/Father uses whatever is at hand to knock on the person's heart. It could be feeding pigs, or it could be a physical accident to you, or a family member leaving. It could be the loss of a job or possibly even some random act of kindness.

The son begins to think. Maybe he should have started thinking a long time before. Just saying. Nevertheless, he did begin to think. His father's farm had better jobs than this job he was doing. So, he begins to reason that he would go back and just work for his father. He would work just as a servant. He thought that he could use his status as a son to get favor from his dad. Here is another gem. We all have built into us a desire to find our Father. Our Creator/Father is good and loving and just waiting for us to return.

Yes, our Creator personally solved all the "free will" and reconnection challenges we caused by our life that ended in "feeding the pigs". Then, He proceeds to come and rescue all of us who will receive His Gift of Love.

We, like the younger son, still try to help God solve our challenges. I will just "work" for my Father. Then He will pay me, and my life will be better. I really don't want to surrender completely, but maybe I will find a compromise. Maybe your compromise is, I will change jobs. Maybe I will change my spouse. Maybe. Maybe. Maybe, I will be better if I change. Anything but complete surrender of my flesh and my ego to my Creator.

## Father Is Sitting on the Porch Waiting for Us to Return

Love (our Creator) is sitting on the porch, waiting for us to turn around and just show up. Also, you need to realize that serving Satan is not fun, and he is a slave master. It will cause you to destroy any good thing in your life. The minute, no, the second we realize that the man Jesus is the way back to our Creator, our Father springs into action. He jumps up and goes to where we are and begins to welcome us home!

Notice that the Father hugs the younger son and will not even let him finish his prepared and rehearsed speech. Another gem: Love does not judge its own. Remember, the reason to choose Jesus is He is the exact version of the Father, and that version is love and family.

Now, we could stop here, as most preaching does, but that would miss some major gems. The gem is that God loves to celebrate! He loves a reason to celebrate and sing for joy when someone chooses to reconnect with Him.

Jesus says: *"I say to you, that there shall be celebration in heaven over one sinner that repents."*

**(Luke 15:7)**

This fact shows that all of the "connected" beings in the spiritual world are vested in the reconnection of the lost children that are in the earthly world. Why is that, you ask? God's family lost one-third of the spiritual beings in Heaven to Lucifer when he convinced them to follow him in his rebellion. (Revelation 12:4)

That was a great loss for God! When we reconnect to Him, we make His loss just a little easier to endure. We make our Creator's day!

Another gem we need to learn is that the "good son" was not good after all. He was proud of his choices. He had been giving to take. He was just as disconnected from his Creator as was the "bad son". The only difference was, he was hiding his motives.

Jesus says it this way: *"God sees not as man sees, for man looks on the outward appearance but the Lord looks on the heart."*

(**1 Samuel 16:7**)

The "good" son's motive was to get all of the praise and his father's estate—just another way of getting what he wanted.

Now for the final gem of knowledge for us in this story. The Father goes and finds the "good son" and reasons with him. He pursues both sons, as both sons need forgiveness and reconnection. This is, in my opinion, unbelievable from an earthly point of view. How could forgiveness be offered to both sons? They both deserve to be disinherited.

That is the beauty of love. It overlooks evil. In fact, Love destroys evil. All any of us must do is accept the gifts of Jesus. And yet some people still ask, why do I need to reconnect with God, our Creator, through Jesus?

We will look at another couple of stories in the Bible and see if there are any more gems for us about our Creator finding His lost children.

LOST AND FOUND

# Chapter 15
# More Lost Are Found!

*A woman having ten silver coins, if she loses one coin does not light a lamp, sweep the house and search carefully until she finds it.*

**(Luke 15:9)**

*What man of you, having a hundred sheep, if he loses one of them, does not leave the ninety-nine in the wilderness, and go after the one which is lost until he finds it?*

**(Luke 15: 4)**

Yes, there are more gems here and evidence Jesus met the conditions of Claim 2. Do you remember what the devil's second claim was? He claimed that God, our Creator, could not and would not forgive people for using their free will to disconnect from our life source. It was this catch-22 where God would not let you be free to choose, because God was mean, and if God let you choose, He would not forgive you anyway! Either way, the Devil trying to create doubt in God.

Now, let's look at more gems from God's word. There are some specific numbers that are important to our Creator. One is 10 and one is 100. Do these numbers symbolize something? And, of course, if they do, Jesus is letting us know He has specific numbers for specific purposes. Maybe He has a specific number of beings He wants to find and reconnect with. Here are some interesting facts about numbers that God wants to show us.

In the Bible, God speaks to the number ten (10) 242 times. The designation "tenth" is used 79 times. Ten is also viewed as a complete and perfect number, as are 3, 7 and 12.

10 is made up of 4, the number of God's first 4 commandments, and 6, the number of commandments about man. As such, 10 signifies testimony, law, responsibility, and the completeness of order.

In Genesis 1, you will find the phrase "God said" 10 times, which is a testimony of His creative power. It is also, in quantum physics, the collapsing of a wave function. God gave the 10 Commandments to man. Ten, therefore, represents man's responsibility to keep the commandments. A tithe is a 10th of our earnings and is a testimony of our faith in Jesus.

The Passover lamb was selected on day 10$^{th}$ of the first month (Exodus 12:3), as was Jesus, the Lamb that takes away the sins of the world. (John 12:28-29; 1 Corinthians 5:7)

Day 10 of the 7$^{th}$ month is also the Holy Day known as the Day of Atonement. This unique day of fasting pictures forgiveness. It also symbolized the removal of

# LOST AND FOUND

Satan, the author of sin, before the millennial reign of Jesus begins. (Revelation 20:1-2)

Wow, the number 10 is very important to our Creator! I am sure that is why Jesus used the story of ten silver coins. In the story, the woman loses 1 of the 10, or 10%. Gem one: God, our Creator, is a God of Order. Nothing is random!

The setting in the story is that the woman is taking inventory of her coins. Now, if she had them in a box and did not use them, I am sure she would not have lost one. What a great observation. The woman is using her coins. Our Creator is working with His Children.

So, upon taking inventory, she discovers she has lost one. What does she do, then? Like every woman, she cleans her house. And to do a proper cleaning, she turns all the lights (lamps) on. Again, she is very serious about finding this lost coin. There is this saying that bad things happen in dark places. Why? Because you can hide things from being discovered in the dark. But when you turn the lights on, what is in the dark is seen and found.

Even after she cleans the house with the lights on, she must still look carefully. Why? Jesus wants to make a point that our Creator is going to look everywhere to find His precious family! You are that important! In the Bible, we are told that Jesus is the Light of the World. As Jesus comes into our physical world of sin and darkness, lost people are exposed.

People that are His are found. Once people are found, they then want to share the free will card available to His lost. Please choose to reconnect. When a found person chooses to reconnect to their Creator, all Heaven is in celebration mode!

Now, what about the number 100? Jesus says, "If any man has a hundred sheep, and one of them goes astray, will he not leave the ninety-nine on the mountains, and go and search for the one that is lost?" (Matthew 18:12)

I think we are going to see something special about the number 100, and still, the lost one is important. The shepherd leaves the saved 99 and goes and looks and does not give up until He finds the one. All Heaven celebrates over the one lost sheep (our Creator's child) who is found.

Jesus is trying to show how important one sheep is! Even when there are 99 people that are reconnected, which some would say is enough. The same message was in the lost coin. Jesus is saying He is not about to lose even one. He wants 100% of His children.

The gem here is, our Creator has no limits on what He will do to save the lost soul. Yes, I used the word soul on purpose. Jesus is here to save people from the second death, the soul death, which comes from God's pressing the delete key on the trash bin on the hard drive (Book of Life) of the Universe. Thank you, Jesus, for saving us!

There are a number of awesome points from these two stories:

- You are the Love of His existence.
- God loves to celebrate
- God will do everything possible to find you
- God does the pursuing, hunting and the finding
- You just need to accept His finding you

Now, let's examine the meaning of the number 100. The meaning can vary depending on the Biblical context in which it is found.

## Abraham Was 100 Years Old When He and Sarah Had Isaac

Abraham was 100 years old (Genesis 21:5), and his wife Sarah was 90 (Genesis 17:17) when Isaac was born. Even though Abraham had already produced a son, Ishmael (through Hagar), God considered Isaac the rightful heir to the promises made to Abraham.

The patriarch Shem, one of Noah's three sons who survived the flood, gave birth to his firstborn son when he was one hundred years old. The birth took place two years after the flood subsided when he was able to leave the ark.

(**Genesis 11:10**)

God promised his people that if they obeyed Him, he would grant them military victories such that five Israelites would be able to overcome one hundred of their enemies. In cases of more numerous opponents, God would cause one hundred children of Israel to be victorious over 10,000 of their enemies.

**(Leviticus 26:7-8)**

There are 39 verses in the Bible that speak to the number 100. In Chronicles 12:14, we are told that the sons of God were equal to 100 of their enemy. In Leviticus 26:8, we are told that 5 sons of Israel will chase 100 and 100 will chase 10,000.

If you continue researching 100, you will find many interesting examples. These examples will show you a thread that our Creator loves math and multiples of 10s and 100s. Again, numbers are important to our Creator, and the most important number is 1. You!

With God doing all the work, the living, the sacrificing, and the pursuing, why does anyone stay lost? Because they do not think they need finding. We will see in the next chapter why lost people don't care that they are lost.

# Chapter 16
# Why Is There a Reconnection Fee?

This is where the answer to claim 2 lies. This is a fundamental question that Lucifer forgot to ask and to answer it, we must ask some other questions. The first question is, "What damage was caused when Adam chose to disconnect from his Creator?"

I mean, it was just a "little" decision. What harm could it have done? No big deal, right? Well, not so fast. We must go back to the creation of Adam.

"What?" you ask. "We've already covered that."

Yes, but I want to make sure you did not miss this point, the point that Adam became a living soul. This was when Adam became a conscious being.

God breathed into Adam, and he became a living soul. That made Adam a spiritual being. He was connected to his Creator through his Creator's spirit. The combination of the Earth and the Spirit created a living soul. However, when he chose to follow the serpent's (Lucifer's) advice, he disconnected his spirit from his Father.

That is why Jesus told Nicodemus that man should be born again to be born of the Spirit. Until man is born again of the Spirit, the damage is done. When Adam made that "little" choice, he affected both his physical body and his spiritual body.

His physical body just began to decay back to dirt. This is like a battery in a flashlight when the light has been left on. The light starts to drain the energy out of it. But because the energy drains slowly, we think that there was and is NO physical effect when we choose to disconnect from our Creator and His life-giving power. And now, because we were born in this condition, we don't know any difference. This is what we inherited from Adam. We just call this slow death normal living. There is a TV show that calls it "the living dead".

However, there is more. The spiritual soul of Adam lost its conscious connection to his creator immediately. That's right. Spiritual separation and death. Right then and right there. Boom. Spiritual separation is an instant event. We are blind to this impact because we do not know any difference. Why? Because as far as we have experienced, we have been born disconnected from our Creator, disconnected from our spiritual life, so we don't know we are separated from our Creator. We have never before experienced the Spirit connection.

Jesus, in talking to Nicodemus, said, *"A man must be born again...born of the spirit and born of the water...before he can enter the kingdom of heaven."*

**(John 3:1-17)**

And, of course, Nicodemus goes physical on Jesus and asks how a man can be born again via his mother. Here is a very learned religious man, and what Jesus is saying goes straight over his head. Wake up, Nicodemus! Jesus is talking about the soul of a man and not his body. This is where we get another clue from Jesus that Adam's decision killed the soul. You cannot be in a found condition without being born again of the Spirit.

## Nicodemus Had a Connection Condition

I am reminded of another story from Jesus in John 12:24-25, when He was talking about a seed. He said, *"Unless a kernel of wheat falls to the ground and dies, it remains just a seed... whoever loves his life will lose it, but whoever hates his life in this world will keep it for eternal life."*

Here is the point: when you are disconnected from your Creator, you will die both of the body and the soul! You must be born again to be transformed into the Kingdom of Heaven. How can you do that? You can't! Yes, we have a problem.

However, not to fear, Jesus is here! Jesus had to take humanity through the journey of dying the second death and being reborn. Then, by His resurrection, He was transforming humanity back into His Creation and into His Kingdom, both physically and spiritually.

Once Adam chooses disconnection, the only way back is through death and then being reborn. But you can't do this for yourself. This action of Jesus was killing Lucifer's idea that there is eternal life apart from God, the idea that the "separated soul" is immortal or even possible. There is no soul life without being connected to God.

## We Must Die and Be Born Again to Enter the Kingdom of Heaven

Pretty simple, right? Then why does everyone refuse to get the point? Why does everyone say, "I want to live just a little apart from God?" What is the big deal?

**Answer**: There is no soul life and no eternal life without being connected to our Creator. Our Creator lives outside of time and space, and this is where the Kingdom of Heaven is found. We think that being physically awake means we are alive and connected to God. **NO.**

Our natural, physically awake state is only related to the Kingdom of this Earth. We see a number of movies these days trying to tell us that our earthly life is eternal. It is a lie! Jesus shows us that you either accept His gift of the payment of the second death or you go through it yourself. Then you will have no life after this world! I suggest you accept Jesus' awesome gift of eternal life.

Now, some of you are starting to get the point, but you want your own connection to God. You think there must be another way, a better way, to connect to God than the man Jesus. You think that your own way back to God is just fine. Just like Cain, you thought that God would be okay with vegetables for an offering. God would understand that he did not have a lamb. God is a loving God, so what is the big deal? You can read that story in Genesis 4:1-6.

Sometimes I am so disappointed with myself. I had to write this book before I really understood. God created Adam to be in a relationship with Him. Adam chooses a relationship with Eve over a relationship with his Creator. Adam chose to disconnect from God. He did not realize that he chose eternal death for both of them, and he would still have to say goodbye to Eve.

Then, a few thousand years later, you come along and say, "I know God, and I can reconnect with God just through myself, my own meditation and prayer." How dumb can you be! You cannot pay the reconnection fee. You cannot die the second death and then come back to life. You cannot create living souls. News flash: you are NOT God! You are a lost soul.

You and I need a second Adam. We need that second Adam to provide us with a new inheritance, an inheritance where we are reborn and connected to our Creator, a new and living way to bring us back to our Creator. Jesus the God Man is the Way.

But of course, you are that Adam! Wow, I wish you would have told me sooner. How foolish of me to miss the fact that YOU are the source of all human life. You, as the Creator, have the ability to pay the reconnection fee for all humanity and then give this reconnection of eternal life to everyone that wants it? I did not realize that you are so loving that you are willing to die to save the whole world! Again, so sorry I misjudged you.

See how foolish that sounds? You cannot reconnect with God yourself. No, we all need a second Adam. And that second Adam is in the form of the man Jesus.

## You Cannot Reconnect with God Yourself?

For those of you who are so proud of yourself that you think you know it all, I will spell it out for you in outline form:

1. Adam's father was God our Creator
2. Adam chose to disconnect from God
3. All humanity came through Adam
4. Adam passed this disconnection state on to the entire world
5. You are a descendent of Adam
6. You are born disconnected from God
7. Therefore, you are lost!

## LOST AND FOUND

There, got it?

Now you **need** the following:

1. Someone who Created you
2. Someone who had God as His direct father
3. Someone who had all humanity in Himself
4. Someone who was and has always been connected to God and is God
5. Someone who has the power to pass this reconnection on to everyone who accepts it
6. You must be able to become a descendent of this Someone
7. This Someone had to have paid the reconnection fee by dying both deaths (going to the second death, a place where God is not) and then coming back to life.
8. Then God's lost children must be able to accept this gift of a new spirit life

This someone is Jesus, our Creator!

Do you believe that? Or do you suffer from a God complex so large that you and Lucifer will be arguing about which of you will be the antichrist?

For the rest of us, all we need to do is accept the life and death and resurrection of Jesus. Here is the miracle. Our rebirth and reconnection are accomplished by a faith connection. By learning of the life, death, and resurrection of Jesus and accepting His gift and His payment for reconnection, we become reborn.

The first Adam gave us Satan and death. The second Adam (Jesus) gave us love and adoption into the family of God, the Kingdom of Heaven, and eternal life.

Now in the next chapter, let us look at the price of the reconnection fee.

# Chapter 17
# The Price of the Reconnection Fee

Let's review: what caused me to be lost? Was it something I did? Was it something that Adam did? Or was it something Lucifer did? Or does it really matter?

The current fact is you (we) are lost. So how do you reconnect to Creator? Well, you die both physically and spiritually and then come back to life. And if, by chance, you could really come back to life, what is the life you would come back to? Since I cannot do all that, how does our Creator do all this for you and me? And then there is still the eternal life question. These are the questions I hope to answer in the next few chapters. Let's start with the question, what caused me to be lost?

### So how do I reconnect to God?

This question can have many different answers if you don't start at the very beginning of the disconnection from our Creator. How do I know when that happened since I was not born yet, you ask? You don't, except for what our Creator has told us Himself and told to a few men, and they wrote their visions down for us to read.

You see, when Adam and Eve were created, their Creator put a tree of free choice in their garden.

**(Genesis 2:15)**

But something else (Satan) was also in the garden. Why was he there? I can't tell you. But I can tell you that there was and is a battle going on between God and Lucifer. Lucifer did not stop at tempting heavenly beings; he went after all God's creations. He brought this war between him and God to our world. He still brings this war to you and me. Someday soon, that war is going to end and when it does, I hope you and I are on the winning side.

Adam and Eve's Creator told them to NOT eat from the tree of free choice, the tree of knowledge of good and evil, or they would die. This was a test to see if they trusted their Creator or not. See, free choice demands that your choice is just that—a free choice. However, free does not mean your choice does not have results. It just means that this free choice is always a condition of God's world.

God wanted all created beings to want and choose to be in relationship with Him. It is no different today in our world, where we want to be with people who want to be with us. Sounds like we were made in the likeness of our Creator.

Adam and Eve were the first ones to have free choice in our world, and they were the first ones that choose to separate themselves from their Creator. The heavenly beings before Adam (beings outside of time and space) had this free choice as well, and yet not all of them chose their Creator. Yep, they wanted to try doing things that were disconnected from their Creator too. They wanted to do things on their own. And the results for them were the same as for Adam and Eve: an instant spiritual separation and death and slow physical death.

Therefore, as they chose to be disconnected from their Creator, they had to leave Heaven and find their own "garden" to live in. Guess what? They chose the same garden as Adam and Eve. Just like in our world, when a couple is happily married, someone tries to move in and split them up, that is what Satan and these disconnected spiritual beings did. They started to bring their "evil god" into our world.

And the rest, as we say, is history. Adam and Eve listened to Lucifer and disconnected from their Creator and all of their offspring were given the inheritance of separation and death. It was so nice of them. And we find that once we are disconnected, on our own, there is no way back!

Yes, on our own, we are incapable of a free will choice back to our Creator. Satan did not tell you that! He did not tell you that once you choose self and disconnect from your Creator, you are a slave to Satan via being a slave to yourself. Yes, now Satan will not let you have free choice. Nope, you are going to exist in his way.

## And the rest, as we say, is history

Reconnection is the only way back, and we were too busy doing things our own way to even be open to learning how to reconnect. This is a pretty helpless condition to be in. We are too busy being the living dead to care to fix the reconnection dilemma, even if we could, which we can't. But not to fear, again, Jesus is here!

Jesus met all the conditions and paid the reconnection price. That price was to leave His heavenly home and His family and go to where they were not. Where is that? The place where only selfish people were. The place where His children would kill His physical body.

He came to our earthly world and then experienced the soul death (second death) at the hands of Satan's helpers, a bunch of lost people. And for Jesus, someone who has spent eternity in the family of love, that is truly a sacrifice.

Jesus was and is the only one who could reconnect humanity. Why was it only Jesus who could reconnect us? The answer is that He was our Creator, and He could create Himself as a human. And through this new form, He could become the same humanity that the first Adam was.

God made Himself in the likeness of Adam and then answered Satan's claims, and by His nature, reconnected all humanity. And God (the Trinity) was His Father. If Jesus did not or could not create people in the first place, then He could not create Himself as the second Adam. In other words, you must have skin in the game to solve these kind of problems.

Jesus had skin in the game. He was our Creator, and He, as the second Adam, is now our redeemer. He started by creating Himself as a baby. Then He lived in our world, always choosing His Father (claim 1). Then dying the soul death, or second death. The real price was to go where His Heavenly family was not. Yes, He paid the price of second death (claim 2). And finally, the rebirth reward of going to get the keys of Hell and Death. In other words, the reconnection or rebirth price is to go to the place where you spiritually die.

Then, He had to raise Himself from being physically and spiritually dead in hell and have the power to give this new life to all humanity who choose this gift. He gave His children a new eternal life in the Kingdom of Heaven! Jesus became a human, lived and died, to do just that for us, so we could have the chance to choose to reconnect to Him. Jesus is the only Being capable of making that happen. That is why Jesus is the Way!

Not only was the reconnection price the highest price to pay, but it required our Creator to pay that price. And He did! But wait, why did Jesus pay the price when He knew most people would not believe He was the answer? And even if they said they believed, they would not give up their stubborn ego? He did it because He loved His family.

Today, we call these people "hokey pokey Christians". One day, they are all in with Jesus, and then the next day, they are all in with the world. This vacillation of their will is just what their ego wants. Remember that once you exercise your "free will" and choose ego (Lucifer), you become a slave to Satan. Then you lose your freedom and your desire to be in a relationship with your heavenly Father.

Paul says in Romans 8, "What I want to do I don't and what I don't want to do I do." This sounds like slavery. So, you must make an "all in with Jesus forever" choice.

But how do you do that? That leads us to the question in the next chapter: which comes first, I am found, or I choose Jesus?

# Chapter 18
# Choice – No Jesus, No Life!

John, one of Jesus's closest friends, tells us that, "while we were yet sinners (lost), Jesus died for us all." Without any connection to the source of life, it is difficult to choose life. Jesus must help us to even want to be found. I think this is perhaps the most obvious fact in my whole book. We are lost with no way to be found without Jesus finding us. Let us look at some of the answers the world is telling us about life.

Our modern world has struggled to find a way to show that life comes from matter. Today, the world knows that is not possible, but for many years, the world thought they had the answer: evolution and the Big Bang.

The world has done many studies to prove life comes from matter. The genome study was just one of many. However, they had no luck with finding the source of life. Conscious life cannot come from physical material.

*"Consciousness is the source of all life!"*

–Dr. Amit Goswami

## Consciousness is not physical

The laws of nature support this fact. Life came from and comes from intelligent design. This belief is built on evidence that matter, the various forms of life, and the entire world were all created by intelligent design. One very simple example is the slugs' felonious feat known as kleptoplasty. It is so remarkable that it's been held up by scientists as proof of *intelligent design*. Yes, a slug!

The point of the theory of evolution is to remove any **purpose** for humanity outside of **random** existence. You just evolved from a tadpole or something. Evolution says you arrived here in this world by chance. Then, of course, you don't have free will, because you were created by random chance. You just evolve by cause and effect, by survival of the fittest, but that theory does not work either. Without intelligent design, you have no reason for free will.

It is not like you had any choice in being here. The universe "farted", and over time you just showed up. Hello there, sunshine! Sooner or later, you and humanity will learn to make the right choice in choosing Jesus, or you will cease to exist. Evolution says there is no purpose for living and no purpose for dying. Life comes, and then life goes. In fact, even humanity will cease to exist given a few billion years or so.

The possibility of this scenario is massively depressing! Here are the facts you need to consider. There are only survival choices in this way of thinking. Choose one way and you die. Choose another way, and you live to make the same choice another day. The only value you have is that you are still alive, if that provides you comfort.

Of course, you are only one choice away from death. And death is defined by the heart not beating and you are only alive when your body and mind has energy flowing through you. When energy leaves your body, you are dead. Life, according to evolution, is all about staying alive. Survival of the fittest or the lucky ones.

Now, consider the transgender movement. It goes right in the face of evolution. Yes, the same people that believe in evolution believe in transgender. But that does not make sense. To survive, you must have a male and a female, or at least for now, you do. Evolutions design is to make sure that humanity survives. But now transgender people say that we don't need genders to survive. These people are going to flat-out kill the human race. That is why they are striving so hard to find a way to sustain life without God's connection. It is amazing that they cannot see the results of their logic.

In fact, just today, I read an article that provides evidence that within 100 years, the population is going to crash upon itself. And when the population starts shrinking, you will not be able to stop it. Then, there will be no survival of the fittest. Just stupid politicians and business people making money via social media. See the article in the epoch times:

https://www.theepochtimes.com/demographers-warn-of-impending-population-collapse_4512821.html?utm_source=ai&utm_medium=search

## Demographers Warn of Impending Population Collapse

We are seeing some countries already starting to implode upon themselves. Russia is just one of them. It takes 2.1 births per death to keep a population stable. Russia is now at 1.3 births per death. The article is very informative as the UN and the International Monetary Fund are telling us just the opposite! By the time we can see who was right, it will be too late. You can do all the transgender surgery you want, but evolution will take over and kill humanity. We better hope there is another way! And there is. Jesus our Creator is the way.

See, if there is no Creator, then there is no right and wrong, just choice for life or choice for death. That is why most people are not alarmed about the abortion crisis or the transgender movement. We just came from a frog, and who cares about an unborn fetus? It will soon be dead anyway, according to evolution. There is no value in human life, as we just came from matter, and that matter is no different than a dog or cat or rat or even a fly.

Without life coming from a Creator, there is no value in life. We are just a random "fart" of the universe. Of course, there is still the question of where matter came from, but never mind that question for now.

## If there is no Creator, then there is no right and wrong

Another fact to consider if we believe we came from matter is the existence of laws. Where did they come from, if not from intelligent design? I know, let's just make up some laws. Then that will give us free choice to obey the law or not. And, of course, we want to have free choice. I am not sure what we want to be free from, but at least it sounds good.

So, a law of a 65 mph speed limit should work. But people break that law all the time. I just saw someone run a red light today, which is a real stupid choice on so many levels. Free choice is not free. If you get caught speeding or running a red light, you will get a ticket or something even worse. That will cost you money and then your insurance will go up. If you continue breaking that law, you will kill someone's child!

Laws of the world are man's attempt to add value to themselves. They want to develop a right or wrong, good or bad. They want to know good and evil. Then we will become as gods. We can add some value to our life. Laws of the land do add value. Finally, a reason for our existence.

But this value is based only upon a law. When you have a law that says please go ahead and kill unborn babies, then who protects the valueless baby? Or who even cares about the valueless baby? Man made laws are only as good as the worst of its people, and there are some pretty valueless people in this world. Maybe if we say these laws are "good", then it will be "good" to kill children.

Just like the chairman of the Federal Reserve said that if we don't kill fetuses, it will make inflation go up. Really, are we now defining "good" by a bank account? Remember, who decides who and what is "good"? The majority or the powerful you?

Not so fast, Jerry, there are many good examples in our world where there are good laws. The majority does make a lot of good laws. The problem is, who influences the majority? Who controls that small rudder that will control the entire ship? A small group of people or Facebook, Instagram, or Twitter can control the whole world. Now the majority is making laws to add value to a few bank accounts. They are telling you this is a good law, but it is just the opposite, and they are making laws for the elite.

But wait again, there are some good people that can really make some good laws, but without there being some intelligent design (Creator), good cannot exist. Good has no value unless it comes from love. Love is the only thing that is good. There is no way for good to exist on its own. There is no point of reference. Why? Because when you just evolved from some tadpole by random choices over vast and unobservable amounts of time, there are only survival choices. Good can only mean I get to live for another day.

We must face the fact that without a Creator, there is no reason to live. Without our Creator setting a value and worth on each one of us, there is no worth—just evolution. And who is in charge of evolution? No one. We need a Creator just to justify why we are here. That is what our Creator wants us to realize.

We are valued by our Creator, who is loving and good. Now finally, we can relax and start to enjoy our life. But wait! We are no longer connected to our Creator. Remember, we choose to be our own gods. We are lost from our source of life and so desperately need and want to be found so we can have value! And with that value, we can have life.

## Without Jesus there is no value in life!

But again, never fear. Jesus our Creator is here! He has made sure that we have free choice to be found. Great! But how did He do it? It means that Jesus put a separation (doubt) between Adam and Eve (humanity) and ego (Lucifer the deceiver). He created a reason for choices, a hidden spark of hope in us. This spark always exists, and it says something is missing. It remains with us as long as we are lost and disconnected from God. We know something is missing, but we just cannot figure it out by ourselves. But the good news from Jesus has told us He has given us a choice.

A clear understanding of what our Creator did for us helps us understand our value. God is eternal. God is energy. God is love. God is our Creator. God has given us a second choice. This is more than reason enough for us to say we have value. Yet we refuse to admit that God is more than matter. We worship matter, and yet it has no life-producing energy. Matter's only value is in being consumed. Matter must be connected to God to keep having energy, to keep growing.

God is willing to stay connected with us if we choose to stay connected to Him. The problem is that we were born disconnected from our Creator. Thanks, Adam! And we do not seem very interested in reconnecting with Him. So, we must go back to the three challenges of God and see that the only way to reconnect is through the Son of God, called Jesus. We will learn more about God the Word and the man Jesus in the next chapter.

For now, it is safe to say that if we are lost, we have trouble valuing ourselves. We are lost and need to be found to value ourselves. We do have that "spark of doubt" within ourselves to be appreciated. Thanks, Jesus! We need to reconnect with our power source, Jesus. The first step: you must realize you are lost. That is a good first step. Then comes the hard part.

We must surrender our ego and ask for forgiveness for our independent choices. We must surrender our "I am going to do it my way." But before you say you can't, let me remind you of the spark of doubt (something is missing) Jesus put in us. That spark is the knowledge that being connected to God is the only way you will have any value at all!

Now, that is good news for us. Disconnection equals my way and no value. Reconnection to our Creator equals God's way and total eternal value!

Let's learn more about this Creator of ours and about His gift of reconnection in the next chapter.

# Chapter 19
# Jesus Always Was and Is and Will Be Eternal

*Truly, truly, I tell you," Jesus declared, "before Abraham was born, I am!*

(John 8:58)

Well, this is a profound statement for so many reasons. First, Abraham lived more than 1767 years before the Man Jesus was born. It does not sound possible for a person listening to Jesus as He makes this statement. The listeners knew who Jesus's parents were and when He was born. Besides, if you just look at Him, you can tell He is under 40 years old. So, Jesus is just making a crazy statement. Plus, would that make Him more special than Abraham even if He was more than 1800 years old? The Bible told of Abraham's direct decedents, and this man was not mentioned, or was He? The Bible did mention there was going to be a Messiah coming someday. Then there is the obvious point that Abraham was the father of all nations and picked by Yahweh, and then he died. What makes this man more special than Abraham, who is dead?

From an earthly point of view, they were correct. But here is the rub—life is more than just an earthly point of view. All of the listeners were materialists. They thought if you couldn't see something, then it was not real. And certainly, they could not see Jesus from a God's point of view. If fact, they wanted to kill Him because they believed Him to be a liar and of the devil. Isn't it odd that they all believed in the devil, and yet they could not see Him from a spiritual point of view? There is something even more important than how these Jews viewed Jesus. Jesus was saying that He was God! He was saying that He was the God—the Word. He was equal to God, the Father. And on top of that, He was the Messiah—the Savior of the world. These words were either true, or Jesus was a liar. And if He was a liar, then there is no Spark of Hope. There is no middle ground here. He is, or He is not God! It is just like Paul said in 1 Cor15:12-22: if God the Word did not raise the Man Jesus from the dead, we are to be pitied the most.

Again, there is no middle ground. Jesus is alive or dead! We are not left to guess. We have many personal eyewitness testimonies declaring they saw Jesus alive! And historians that lived within 150 years of Jesus supported that Jesus existed. First, let us see what some historians say about Jesus. This will answer the "doubters" who say that Jesus is only spoken about in the Bible. From those writers, we can learn more than 12 things about Jesus without opening a Bible. The reference to those documents is in my appendixes.

This fact was reported by Jewish Historian Josephus, who was born around AD 37. In his *Antiquities of the Jews*, he reports:

*At this time there was a wise man named Jesus. His conduct was good, and [he] was known to be virtuous. (1)*

In recounting the stoning of James, Josephus records:

*So, he assembled the Sanhedrin of judges, and brought before them the brother of Jesus, who was called Christ, whose name was James, and some others; and when he had formed an accusation against them as breakers of the law, he delivered them to be stoned. (2)*

Celsus was a 2$^{nd}$-century Greek philosopher and a fierce opponent of Christianity. In what is known to be the first comprehensive intellectual attack on Christianity, he tried to resolve why Jesus was able to perform miracles. The story is wild—but the main point is that by trying to explain away the miracles of Jesus, he is actually affirming that they happened:

*Jesus, on account of his poverty, was hired out to go to Egypt. While there he acquired certain powers which Egyptians pride themselves on possessing. He returned home highly elated at possessing these powers, and on the strength of them gave himself out to be a god.(3)*

This fact comes to us from one of the most trusted historians of the ancient world. Cornelius Tacitus was born in AD56 and served as a respected senator and proconsul of Asia under Emperor Vespasian. He wrote a history of the first-century Roman Empire, which many historians consider to be the "pinnacle of Roman historical writing."(4) He notes:

*Christus, from whom the name had its origin, suffered the extreme penalty during the reign of Tiberius at the hands of one of our procurators, Pontius Pilatus. (5)*

**Josephus confirmed:**

*Pilate condemned him to be crucified and to die. (6)*

This fact was originally recorded by a Samaritan historian named Thallus, who was alive at the same time Jesus was (AD 5-60). He wrote a 3-volume history of the 1st-century Mediterranean world, which unfortunately no longer exists. But before his writings were lost, he was cited by another ancient historian, Julius Africanus, in AD 221. Africanus described Thallus' account of what happened during Jesus' crucifixion:

*On the whole world there pressed a most fearful darkness; and the rocks were rent by an earthquake, and many places in Judea and other districts were thrown down. (7)*

**Josephus wrote:**

*And many people from among the Jews and the other nations became his disciples. Pilate condemned him to be crucified and to die. And those who had become his disciples did not abandon discipleship. (8)*

Julius Africanus also reported that another ancient historian, Phlegon, confirmed the darkness at the time of Jesus' death and that Jesus was alive "in the time of" Tiberius Caesar:

*Phlegon records that, in the time of Tiberius Caesar, at full noon, there was a full eclipse of the sun from the sixth hour to the ninth. (9)*

In his commentary regarding the disciples' reaction to Jesus' death, Josephus recorded:

*[Jesus' disciples] reported that He had appeared to them three days after his crucifixion; and that he was alive.... (10)*

Pliny the Younger lived from AD 61-113 and was an influential lawyer and magistrate of ancient Rome. In a letter to Emperor Trajan, he wrote:

*They [Christians] were in the habit of meeting on a certain fixed day before it was light, when they sang in alternate verses a hymn to Christ, as to a god, and bound themselves by a solemn oath, not to any wicked deeds, but never to commit any fraud, theft or adultery, never to falsify their word, nor deny a trust when they should be called upon to deliver it up. (11)*

Lucian of Samosata was a 2nd-century Greek satirist known for his wit and sarcasm. Even though Christians were the object of his snark, he affirmed certain details about them:

*The Christians, you know worship a man to this day—the distinguished personage who introduced their novel rights and was crucified on that account....it was impressed on them by their original lawgiver that they are all brothers, from the moment that they are converted, and deny the gods of Greece, and worship the crucified sage, and live after his laws.* (12)

Suetonius recorded the persecution and suffering of early Christians, the official secretary of the Roman Emperor Hadrian, around AD 121. He documented that they were expelled from Rome in AD 49 by Claudius:

*Because the Jews at Rome caused constant disturbances at the instigation of Chrestus (Christ), he expelled them from Rome.* (13)

*Nero inflicted punishment on the Christians, a sect given to a new and mischievous religious belief.* (14)

Tacitus also confirmed Nero's persecution of early Christians:

*Nero fastened the guilt and inflicted the most exquisite tortures on a class hated for their abominations, called Christians by the populace.* (15)

Wow, I would be surprised if you realized how many non-Christians confirmed that Jesus was alive, performed miracles, and rose from the dead! Today we have a legal system that is built on eyewitnesses. Let us look at some eyewitness testimonies to hear what they saw. First, Paul saw Jesus. He says that Jesus appeared to him in 1 Cor 15:8. Paul was a well-educated man known to tell the truth. Plus, he was so convinced that "the Christians" were bad that he spent years trying to kill them. Then one day, Paul got knocked off his donkey. Jesus appeared to him <u>after</u> Jesus went back to heaven, and that experience changed his life.

Note: All of us will sooner or later have a "knocked off your donkey" experience. Trust me, I had one and recommend that you listen to Jesus before that happens to you too. I will tell you more about that experience in a future chapter.

Paul's experience is significant because this was after Jesus returned to heaven! At least five times, including Paul's experience, the bible mentions people seeing Jesus after He returned to heaven. First, He appeared to Stephen as he was being stoned in 36 AD (Acts 7:55). And Saul (Paul) was watching the stoning of Stephen. Next, in 36 AD, Paul was on the road to Damascus (Acts 9:1-19). Then in 36AD, Jesus appeared to Saint Ananias, telling him to go and heal Paul (Acts 9:10-18). Then Jesus again appeared to Paul in the temple to warn him of trouble that was coming (Acts 22:17-21). And finally, to John on the isle of Patmos to show John the visions that are written in the book of Revelation (Rev 1:1).

I know I am getting ahead of myself because I am so excited with the evidence Jesus gives us that He arose from the dead and is alive! The evidence began when Jesus appeared to Mary Magdalene. (Mark 16:9-11) (John 20:11-18) Then He appeared to the men walking to Emmaus. (Mark 16:12-13) (Luke 24:13-35). Then He appeared to Peter in Luke 24:34. Then He appeared to the ten disciples in the upper room. (Luke 24:36-49) And then later, Jesus appeared to the 11 disciples (He did not want to leave out Thomas) in the same upper room. (Mark 16:14-18) (John 20:26-29) (1 Cor 15:5). Then Jesus went fishing with the seven disciples on the lake of Galilee. (John 21:1-23).

**Jesus appeared to more than 500 people after His resurrection.**

Then Jesus appeared to more than 500 people after His resurrection. (1 Cor 15:6). After that, He saw His brother James. (1 Cor 15:7) Jesus spent 40 days visiting friends, family, and His disciples. This is the same time He spent in the wilderness of temptation. His first objective was to explain the Old Testament prophecies to them. Showing them all the different verses that mention His coming, death, and resurrection. He was setting the table for their life after He went back to Heaven. Also, He promised them He would send them the Holy Spirit. (More on the Holy

Spirit later). And then all the disciples saw Him go up into the Heavens to His Father. Acts 1: 9-11.

I think the time Jesus spent on this earth after His resurrection was very significant. Let's look at some of the facts. Jesus likes 40 days. It seems that it is a very important timeline to God. But before we look at the 40 days, let us look at some more evidence of when Jesus appeared to people after His ascension. You may say I did not know that Jesus appeared to anyone after the disciples. Well, this may come as a surprise that we have documented testimony of more than 25 times that Jesus appeared to people after His Resurrection. It also says that many "graves were opened", and people were raised from the dead and went into the holy city and appeared unto many. (Matthew 27:52-53). Can you imagine if you buried your grandfather 30 years ago, and he just one day knocks on your door? Or maybe John the Baptist knocks on your door.

As I said earlier, our laws today say on the evidence and testimony of 2 or more people— the truth is confirmed. Well, considering the evidence, it is fair to say from all these testimonies that Jesus is alive and well. He is living somewhere outside of "time and space" in The Kingdom of Heaven, as Jesus called it. And yet He is able to re-enter "time and space" to appear to His people. Sometimes Jesus will even appear to someone that does not believe in Him just to "knock that person off their donkey."

## LOST AND FOUND

These are the same facts that we use to prove science. Can we observe the event, and can an observer measure it? The answer is *yes*. Here is the rub. People say that if "they" are not the observer themselves, then Jesus does *not* exist. To them, I must ask, have you been to the moon? Have you observed the "double-slit" experience? Have you seen the splitting of the atom? How about something as simple as electricity? Of course, most of you have not. And yet you still believe in those things. Why? Because someone else has observed the event. In chapter 25, I will provide even more evidence as to why it is smart to believe.

Now, let's look at some of the 40-day events and look for any 40-day patterns. Of all the Old Testament types and patterns, none is more amazing than the 40-day pattern as it continues to point to the fulfillment of Promises. What do I mean by Promises? Many 40-day events in the Bible ended with Promises. The first of these 40-day events happened at the time of the flood— "it rained for 40 days and 40 nights" (Gen 7:4). The second is when Moses was on Mount Sinai for 40 days talking with God the Word (Jesus) Exodus 24:18.

Some more were when the spies that went to check out the land of Canaan spent 40 days searching out the land (Numbers 13:25). Goliath presented himself to Israel for 40 days before David killed him (1 Samuel 8:28). Elijah had one meal from the angel, and it lasted him for 40 days (1 Kings 19:8). Ezekiel bore the iniquity of the house of Judah for 40 days (Ezekiel 4:6). God gave Nineveh 40 days to repent

(Jonah 3:4). Jesus was tempted for 40 days (Luke 4:2), and of course, Jesus was on the earth for 40 days before He went back to Heaven (Acts 1:3). All of these events ended with a Promise. Some, like the 40 days that God gave Nineveh to repent, would end in either a crisis of fire or forgiveness from God. Either way, there was a Promise. Forty days of rain during the flood ended with a Promise from God to never destroy the earth again by water. We are reminded of that promise today by the rainbow. This period represents a testing time. After this period of time passes, God's promise of judgment comes. Sometimes a good judgment and sometimes not so good is performed on the world.

The 40 days that Jesus spent on this earth before He left our earth was a sweet and sour time. Yes, He appeared to many people to make sure they all knew He was alive. But it ended with Him leaving and giving us the Holy Spirit. Yes, it was very sad to see Jesus leave.

But wait, He gave them two promises. First, in Acts 1:11, He will return for us. Second, He would send us all His Holy Spirit! John 14:15-31 Jesus ensured that His earthly family would be cared for. How? His "Presence" was sent in the form of Conscious Energy, i.e., the Holy Spirit, to lead us into all *truth* and provide us with all *wisdom*. Why do I know that? Jesus said that this Spirit would be a life-changing event. Yes, by the Spirit, our lives would be changed forever. By the "Spirit," we could now be "born again." (John 3:3,5)

## LOST AND FOUND

We could have the "Spark" and be convicted of being "lost" by the Holy Spirit. (John 16:7-11) We would be "led into all Truth" by the Spirit. (John 16:13). Yes, Jesus said we must be born again of the Spirit to have Eternal Life, and then He gives us the Spirit so we can be born again! This "born again" is exercising our choice to reconnect to our Creator. Just one more gift from Jesus to make sure we have Eternal Life.

Eternal Life is Spiritual. Eternal Life is Spirit and Consciousness. Eternal Life is never ending Energy. And we know that Energy *cannot* be created or destroyed. It can only change its state. God must change our state from a physical form of life to a spiritual form of life. Welcome to the Kingdom that is not of this world (John 18:36). Welcome to the Kingdom of Heaven.

Of course, some of you will ask what keeps me from changing my state myself. Why can't I just change my state from a physical state to a spiritual state by changing my own thoughts? Really, you want to ask that question again? That takes us back to our creation. God the Word "breathed" into Adam, and he became a living soul.

You cannot change your state without the "breath" (Spirit) of our Creator, which you choose to separate from. I hope I have shown you that anything your ego asks is death. To quote Bob Newhart, just "Stop It!" Stop thinking you can do it yourself! Back to the gift of His Spirit. Jesus had taken our human physical form on Himself. Why? He needed to become the second Adam, and then He could reconnect all lost humanity back to Himself. *Awesome!* Thank you, Jesus!

But that sacrificial act of our "God the Word" to become the Man Jesus limited Himself in some future forms. He chooses to give up His Spirit. No worries, Jesus had the answer. I will send you My Holy Spirit (Acts 1:1-5), so you will have more than just the Man Jesus. What do you mean, Jesus? Well, when Jesus set aside His "God the Word" form, He left His Spirit in the Father. And now Jesus is sending that Holy Spirit to us. Just one more thing God planned from "before the foundation of the world." (Ephesians 1:4)

This Good news of His Spirit is Jesus was preparing to share His Spirit with everyone who wants their name written in the Book of Life. That was exactly what Jesus and the two angels told the disciples. Jesus said, "Go and make disciples of all nations, baptizing them in the name of the Father and of the Son and of the Holy Spirit." (Matthew 28:16-20). The Holy Spirit was the way Jesus was going to "seek and save those that were lost." (Luke 19:10). So far, we have learned quite a bit about our Creator (God the Word) and His Science. In the next chapter, we will learn about the Man Jesus and His Science.

# Chapter 20
# Jesus said: "I am the Way" – (John 14:6)

"Why do I need to believe in Jesus? I have my own connection with God." "I believe in God, but this Jesus, I don't see why I need to believe in Him?" "I am a good person and as long as I live my life the best way possible, I can get whatever reward is on the other side of this life." I hear these kinds of comments repeatedly, and most of the time, they all sound the same. It's like people saying 2+2 is whatever they want it to be. Just because we say something is true does not make it true, right?

The Man Jesus is the same being as God, or He is not. You either believe Jesus and what he is telling as the truth, or you are calling Him a liar. There are no two ways about it. The Bible says, "Even the Devil believes", so why don't you? Are you smarter than Lucifer? Sounds like you have already made up your mind that you are your own god, and you are calling yourself god in the unseen world. Always remember, our Creator says pride comes before a fall.

We may say that we have eternal life. But that's not true unless you stay connected to someone or some being that is eternal. Without which, you will physically die as your battery (body) ages and loses energy. You cannot have the way to eternal life through yourself. Life is sustainable only if we stay connected to our Creator.

You are already spiritually dead from birth because you are already disconnected from your Creator and if you learn the truth and still choose to deny Jesus and His Gift, you will remain dead from within. We must see that Jesus is our Creator and He is the only source of eternal life. If you still think you can live without Him, then you might as well join the people who believe the earth is flat.

Let us look back to Jesus after His Resurrection. In Chapter 19, we learned that there were more than 500 observers that saw Jesus after He came back to life. In fact, many of these same observers also tell us Jesus is the Creator and the source of life.

> *"He was with God in the beginning. Through him all things were made; without him nothing was made that has been made. In him was life, and that life was the light of all mankind."*
>
> **(John 1:2-4)**

Science tells us that the universe was designed Intelligently. We can keep going over the same arguments, but if you do not believe by now, then you may never believe in the miracles of Jesus and God who created this divine universe, which is beyond our comprehension.

# LOST AND FOUND

In Chapter 4, we learned that our Creator and God the Word had three challenges to solve from Lucifer's questions of doubt and rebellion. We learned that these three problems centered around "free choice" and the perceived changes of leadership in Heaven. We also learned that our God the Word had an answer to all these problems. In fact, it would be our God the Word that would solve all three problems in the form of the Man Jesus.

Remember we inherited our "lost condition" from Adam.

The solution was that God the Word was to take human form and become the Man Jesus, our second Adam. This is where faith comes into play. We cannot observe the unseen world. We cannot observe God the Word anymore. Our choices separated us from our Creator, and in our lost and separated state, we were restricted from seeing spiritual things. We are like the disciple Thomas when he said,

"Unless I see the scars of the nails in his hands and put my finger on those scars and my hand in his side, I will not believe" He had the "I must see it to believe it" philosophy. This belief limits a person. If you only depend upon your eyes for reality, then you are mostly blind. Our God the Word knew our condition and limitations that is why He left His place in the unseen world and entered our world via a virgin birth.

Can you imagine how Mary must have felt when the Holy Spirit told her she was going to give birth to baby Jesus? Just one day, you become pregnant with just a feeling that the Spirit "overshadowed" you. That is what happened to Mary. Witnesses of this event would be good to hear from. First, Mary, then Joseph, her husband, then Elizabeth and other family members, the list goes on and on. Some of them are listed in the Bible, and some are historians.

Here is where we see the uniqueness of the Man Jesus. He had His Father's (God of the Spirit's) DNA and his mother, Mary's physical DNA. The only other person that had a spiritual and earthly DNA mixture was first Adam. The first Adam also had an advantage over the second Adam because his physical DNA had not been conditioned to fleshly desires. And yet, with the first Adam, it did not end so well. Let's hope the second Adam – The Man Jesus ends up better than the first Adam.

No pressure, Man Jesus!

Jesus had to live with free will and earthly DNA that had been conditioned by 4,000 years of fleshly desires and corruption. But He always chooses to live with God's love, the spiritual connection to life's energy and to the will of God the Father who remained in the unseen world. This was a very challenging task! Why? Earth's DNA is not in agreement with the spiritual DNA. Ego cannot live with love because ego wants what ego wants!

## LOST AND FOUND

God's spiritual DNA wants to love what God wants to love. Jesus said that it is impossible to serve both God (Love) and money (Ego). Love is the only way to the eternal energy connection. Without a love connection with God, there is no eternal life. And if the Man Jesus chose His own ego for even a second, then Lucifer's claim in doubt problem #1 would have been right. The love connection would have just been a theory and nothing more.

The Man Jesus must travel through time, meeting all the challenges presented by Mr. Ego (Lucifer). Jesus was an overachiever and motivated by love! He started from birth and went all through his life, meeting challenges. He did not let even one single challenge by Satan slip by Him. He met them all and always chose to stay connected to love's energy connection and His Father's will. This is evidence enough to support Jesus's claim in John 17 that He was and is always connected to the Father. Trust me, Lucifer would have argued with God if he could have that Jesus choose His own way.

There is more to this battle than it seems. The battles of the physical world were just the beginning. I know that is all you can see, but that is not where the real challenges and battles are. A great example of this is found in the events of 2 Kings 6:17-20.

And Elisha prayed and said, "Lord, I pray, open his eyes that he may see." Then the Lord opened the eyes of the young man, and he saw. And behold, the mountain was full of horses and chariots of fire all around Elisha. So, when the Syrians came down to him, Elisha prayed to the Lord, and said, "Strike this people, I pray, with blindness." And He struck them with blindness according to the word of Elisha.

Now Elisha said to them, "This is not the way, nor is this the city. Follow me, and I will bring you to the man whom you seek." But he led them to Samaria.

So it was, when they had come to Samaria, that Elisha said, "Lord, open the eyes of these men, that they may see." And the Lord opened their eyes, and they saw; and there they were, inside Samaria!

Elisha was a prophet, and he had a servant. They were in a city in Israel, and the Philistines were attacking them. The servant was sure they were dead. Elisha prayed to the God the Word (our Creator) and asked that the servants' eyes be opened.

The Servant's eyes were opened to the spiritual world. When you can see into the spiritual world, you see a completely different reality! Not only were they going to live, they were going to defeat their earthly enemy. However, without having a spiritual connection to God, you cannot see anything spiritual. You only see darkness and hopelessness. With spiritual eyesight, you see truth and victory. God the Word became the Man Jesus and brought spiritual victory to a lost world. That is what you see with spiritual eyesight.

In recap, Mr. Ego doubt challenge #1 was solved by the Man Jesus but remember, Mr. Ego had a doubt challenge #2. It was about paying the reconnection price to allow lost humanity to be reconnected to the love energy of our Creator. This reconnection must be solved in the spiritual world because the only way to reconnect the body to the spirit world is through the death of the physical body—death of the ego. This is another law of the universe; new life comes via the death of the old body. A simple example is of the seed. It dies to be alive again and bring abundance with it.

When we talk about death, which death are we talking about? The passing of the body or of the spirit or both? Being dead, both physically and spiritually, means there is no return to either world. It's something Lucifer missed in his gamble. No one had died, both physically and spiritually and come back to the Kingdom of Heaven. So, Lucifer thought that there was life after physical death where he would become the god of all these half-dead beings. If you are not the source of life, you make all kinds of stupid choices and assumptions. But how do the Man Jesus and God the Word solve this death issue to bring life back to all of His Creation?

The right question is; Is there a place in the universe where God doesn't exist? Most of us would say no because we have been told that God is everywhere. However, Jesus tells us there is one place where God doesn't exist. He calls it Sheol.

In Revelation 1:18, we learn that Jesus went to Sheol and took the keys of hell and death during his second death experience. So, when Jesus appeared to Mary upon His Resurrection, He said to her to not touch Him as He had not been to His Father yet. He was doing something in the spiritual world when the physical world thought He was dead.

Another question arises; Is the unseen world more real than the seen?

## LOST AND FOUND

Jesus was busy fixing the reconnection of the lost race to their divine connection when everyone thought that Lucifer had won by killing Jesus God's Solution to Satan's doubt challenge #2. Without the Man Jesus alive, there would be no answer to the reconnection challenge, and Lucifer would have won. Not so fast, Lucifer, the Man Jesus was dead, but God the Word was alive and well. He was recreating His live connections with His creations, paying the price that no one else could pay - the Reconnection Fee Price.

"For the wages of sin is death, but the gift of God is eternal life in Christ Jesus our Lord." (Romans 6:23)

And then you ask, why do I need Jesus for eternal life?

Jesus has the keys of Hell and Death!

Now, there is only one more challenge left. How does the Man Jesus get the Human Race to realize that they now have a chance to choose life again? This is going to take some time! Jesus had a plan, but so did Lucifer. Who do you think is going to win? A creature of God who is separated from the life source or the Creator of all life? Is that even a question? But think again; humans love their ego, and that ego keeps most of them from choosing Jesus. They love being their own gods in the physical world!

Humans are lost and separated from God. They like to pretend they are not lost and continue to live in the darkness of this physical world. They are an easy mark for Lucifer. In fact, they don't need any encouragement to live as their own Gods. Humans are quite content to be their own gods. They just accept this is the way things are, and they need to accept the facts of life and make the best of it; Just be good people. That sounds reasonable enough to lost People.

God needed to develop a strategy to solve His challenge #3. How to reach humans with the Good News that the Man Jesus and God the Word had solved both of Lucifer's challenges! Just tell them that Jesus is giving us all this Reconnection for free! All people have to do is believe and accept His free gift, and you will have eternal life. Sounds really easy.

Who wouldn't want this free gift? You would think everyone would want Eternal Life? Most people do NOT want eternal life. Here is an amazing fact; they do not want eternal life if it means giving up being their own god!

Humans are so in love with their own way that they refuse to accept the better way of life. Who can blame them? Humans have done such a good job of managing life on this planet that they don't consider change at all. Why change now? Just give them 20 more years, and they will have everything fixed. They will fix all the marriage problems, gender problems, and social media problems. Humans are so in love with themselves, they will keep choosing present life to the possibility of a much better future.

# LOST AND FOUND

Here are just a few examples of how good of a job we have done making this world a better place:

The slave trade children, the pervs, the universal drug addictions, the rapes and pillaging are just a few things that humans have been successful in handling, not! After all, this world is not going to last forever, so we might as well get while the getting is good. Too bad for the thousands of species that have already died, all thanks to humans. I have only spoken of three issues in our world, and you still don't want to learn about God's Good News?

So, are you interested in hearing about God's plan to spread the Good News? Anyone in their right mind would want something better than what this world has to offer. All it takes is giving up on "your way" and accepting the gift that the Man Jesus, God the Word, your Creator, is offering for free. What do you have to lose? Pascal answers that question in his writing on "Pascal's Wager", which we will discuss later. He really does tell you that you have NOTHING to lose in choosing God.

## Chapter 21
## "Fear not, for behold, I bring you good news" – (Luke 2:10)

Is there a solution to our world's problems that works for EVERYONE? One answer that solves all problems, big or small? Before we get into finding this golden solution that fixes all our problems, let's identify what needs fixing. The usual answers to this question are:

- My life
- My job
- My marriage
- My house
- My lack of savings
- My child
- My height
- My weight
- My health

The list is never-ending. It's clear that we have problems, and even though we had been living with these issues almost all our lives, now we need prompt solutions. In fact, we need to know where to find answers because we have lost our way. It's because we have been looking for solutions in the wrong place. It's when we turn to Jesus for solution, we hear his words loud and clear:

- I came to seek and save those that were lost
- I am the living water
- I am the light of the world
- I am the Prince of Peace
- I am the joy to the world
- I am the everlasting Father
- I am the King of Kings
- I am the beginning and the end
- I am the first and the last
- I am patient and long-suffering
- I am eternal life
- I am love
- I am the way!

His words sound enthralling. They give us hope that there is an answer to all of our problems. Let us take a look at Jesus's life when He was here on this earth to see how He is going to fix everything. How did He help people when He was here? Remember, He came to this world to solve 3 challenges. And while He was solving the "big three", He also managed to find time to help people. The Bible is full of examples, but we will look at just a few.

Let us start at the beginning of His ministry. His first miracle was turning water into wine. Jesus said to the servants, "Fill the jars with water"; so they filled them to the brim. Then he told them, "Now draw some out and take it to the master of the banquet." They did so, and the master of the banquet tasted the water that had been turned into wine. (John 2:1-11.)

This was just to make his mother happy. She said, "Whatever He says, DO IT". There is our answer. After his mother was happy, Jesus proceeded to take the next 3 ½ years, making other people happy.

Here is a list of some of His miracle healings:

- Lepers cleansed: Matthew 8:1–4; Mark 1:41–45; Luke 5:12–14; 17:11–19.
- Blind receive sight: Matthew 9:27–31; Mark 8:22–26; Luke 18:35–43; John 9:1–38.
- People are healed from a distance: Matthew 8:5–13; Luke 7:2–10; John 4:46–54.
- Peter's mother-in-law healed: Mark 1:29–31.
- Paralyzed man healed: Matthew 9:1–8; Mark 2:1–12; Luke 5:17–26.
- People touching Jesus' clothing are healed: Matthew 9:20–23; 14:35–36; Mark 5:25–34; 6:53–56; Luke 8:43–48.

- Various healings on the Sabbath just to make the point that Sabbath was man for man and not man for the Sabbath: Mark 3:1–6; Luke 6:6–10; 13:10–17; 14:1–6; John 5:1–18.
- Deaf and mute man healed: Mark 7:31–37.
- Cut-off ear is repaired: Luke 22:47–53.
- Demons cast out (and specific physical ailments accompanying the demons healed): Matthew 9:32–33; 17:14–18; Mark 9:14–29; Luke 9:37–42.
- Demons cast out (no specific physical ailments mentioned): Matthew 8:28–34; 15:21–28; Mark 1:23–27; 5:1–20; 7:24–30; Luke 4:31–37; 8:26–39.
- Multitudes healed where Jesus did not even meet all the people. Kind of like a group healing: Matthew 9:35; 15:29–31; Mark 1:32–34; 3:9–12; Luke 6:17–19.
- Then the make the point that He was the Creator God He raised the dead to life: Matthew 9:18–26; Mark 5:21–43; Luke 8:40–56; John 11:1–45.

Jesus did more than heal people. Some of his other significant miracles are:

- Jesus feeds (3,000 and 5,000 at a time): Matthew 14:13–21; 15:32–39; Mark 6:33–44; 8:1–10; Luke 9:12–17; John 6:1–14
- Jesus walks on water: Matthew 14:22–33

- Jesus makes Peter walk on water: Mark 6:45–52; John 6:15–21
- Jesus calms a storm: Matthew 8:22–25; Mark 4:35–41; Luke 8:22–25
- Jesus fills nets with fish twice: Luke 5:1–11; John 21:1–14
- Jesus has Peter catch a fish with money in its mouth (for the temple tax): Matthew 17:24–27
- Jesus cursed the fig tree and it withers: Matthew 21:18–22; Mark 11:12–25
- Jesus turns water to wine - His first miracle: John 2:1–11

We clearly see that the nature of Jesus was to help people. That is why He said I came to seek and SAVE those who are lost. Remember, we have established that you were born lost, or do you still think you are fine on your own? We actually know this answer after going through 20 chapters. But it is good to remind ourselves that we need Jesus! We do need to be found, and with Jesus, our lives will be much better!

Jesus performed miracles to get everyone's attention. "Because God is kind, because his kindness is rich, because he's patient. His kindness leads you toward repentance - Romans 2:4. Repentance means a change of mind. But that was just the beginning. His plan was to convince people about rebirth, that they needed to be born again, to be born of the spirit, to move from the physical world to the spiritual world, to die to self and to be born of the spirit. Jesus said to Pilate that His kingdom was not of this world. His goal was to reconnect lost people of this world to their Creator in the Spirit World and this is what a spiritual rebirth or reconnection is called. That spiritual world is where Jesus wants to take His children. He calls it the Kingdom of Heaven.

Again, Jesus came and lived a "free" life and always choose His Father's will. Then He died his $2^{nd}$ death. Why? So, He could give Eternal Life to all those who accept His free gift. Then He came back to life and spent 40 days showing people that His Victory over death and sin and Satan was won. And this victory is free to ALL people.

While He was preparing to leave, He made one major announcement and one major command. The announcement: He was coming back! And even though He was leaving, He would come back and take us all who believe in Him to the spiritual world of Eternal Love—to the Lost Kingdom of Heaven.

Then He told us to share this Good News with His lost children all over the world. He wants us to follow His example in sharing this News. We were to be creative and use different ways to reach different people. Here is a fun fact about our Creator. He made over 16,000 different types of butterflies to occupy the country of Panama, which means our Creator likes uniqueness. There needs to be as many different ways to reach people who are lost as there are lost people.

Why would you not want this? We all must find ways to tell the lost people how they can be found. That is the last of the 3 challenges of Jesus that is left in this physical world. God's challenge #3 -  people must find Jesus. Finding Jesus is easy when you admit you are lost. It gets difficult when you don't think you are lost, and you do not need Jesus. Mr. Ego keeps most of the world lost and in his control. The world is designed to keep people busy in achieving material success.

We need a better paying job, better bank account, bigger and better house, faster car, better suntan, better vacation, better job, more power, and more of this physical life because that is all there is to life. At least, that's what we believe. Lucifer lies to you by insinuating that God did not give you enough, so you need to take more, more, more. He says that with the right man, the right woman, the right job, the right house, you will find happiness and success. So, you need to spend all your life pursuing things of this world, sparing no time to even consider life after death. This world and his lie has got you as a captive.

This is where we are today.  We are trying to show most everyone that they are lost. Most people are not even interested in the spiritual World. We are showing them that Jesus has already found them and taken them with Him into the spiritual world in Himself. The only thing left is for lost people to accept what He had done for all of them. Maybe some will hear the message and choose Jesus. He has one more surprise - He promises to make sure everyone will have at least one conscious choice by putting a "get out of jail" card in everyone's wallet.

Remember the ad that says, "what's in your wallet"? You have one ticket in your wallet that He promised you from the beginning. He said the ticket is, "I will put enmity (disagreement) between the devil's seed and God's children. God will, sooner or later, cause an event that will make you choose Him or the world. This 'get out of jail' card is our safety net for being found. It is the only card we need in our wallet of life.

As I have said over and over, we inherited our "lost condition" from Adam. This lost condition is where the devil wants to keep us. In that condition, we are "food" for the spiritual beings. "Satan is a roaring lion seeking whom he can devour" (1 Peter 5:8). If we don't know we are lost, then we can't use the "salvation card".

In fact, these lost people will think we are stupid when we say they are lost. We have talked about this several times in this book. People think their own personal condition is the normal way of life. We don't even think there is a problem until we experience a lost condition of this world. WWII was just one of many examples of the lost condition of the world.

We have this card that tells us something is not right. However, with our ego as god, we come up with some pretty crazy answers for evil. Most answers involve some "power" move. We seem to think that we can force people to "do good". What we don't get is that without our connection to the Creator, all of our answers to evil are just dumb.

Here is an example: Hitler kills millions of Jews in the gas chamber. The USA just dropped a nuclear bomb on Japan that killed thousands. Russia attacked Ukraine just to warn NATO. All of these behaviors contain no love and grace. That is why Jesus gave us the "get out of jail" card. It is a small but powerful thought that lives inside everyone. This thought means there is a better way - a Divine Way. Now, we can reject that thought and turn back to our own ego. But every now and then, someone entertains this Divine Way and immediately that person is found. This process of being found is what Jesus did with His life on this earth. Yes, our answer came from the spiritual world. The answer for us, in the physical world, is Jesus.

Jesus says, "I am the way, the truth and the life". This is the Good News!

As we live in this world, we see all kinds of evil. We see child abuse, lying, cheating, deceiving and even murder. Our goal, as people who have been found, is to use the evil in the world to show Jesus has a better way. This better way is something more than just enough food, enough money, and enough safety. This better way is a "new heart"! A

# LOST AND FOUND

death to Mr. Ego and a new life connected to Jesus. That is when a love connection to Jesus becomes our way of life.

Jesus has done everything to cause us to be found! This good news is just what a "lost" world needs. Let's continue to explore new ways to help people see that they are lost. If you live in darkness, is it possible to see that you are lost? You just cannot see without light! Again, Jesus says, "I am the light of the world". We must leave our ego at the door and choose Jesus. That is the Good News.

Finally, we have been found!

# Chapter 22
# I Had No Idea There Are so Many Lost People

When my son quit smoking, he became very critical of smokers. Everywhere he looked, someone was smoking. It was beginning to drive him crazy. I tried to tell him that he was one of those smokers just a few months earlier. I told him that he just saw life differently now that he had quit smoking. So, he began to change his focus and decided to help smokers quit smoking. He went from being critical to wanting to help people.

Here is another viewpoint to consider. When you buy a car, you start seeing that same car on the streets. You may have remarked, "I cannot believe so many people are driving the same car as me." This is very similar to being "found". When you're found, everyone else seems lost to you. We need to develop a way to communicate with these people. We need to find ways to show them Jesus. And then that He is the light and that light will show them the way to be found.

Step one is to stop and look at what people are doing. You may ask the question. Are there any common traits of lost people? Let us turn to the Bible for some answers. The Bible says there are two major groups of people in God's Family.

# LOST AND FOUND

1. Children of God, our Creator, that are of this world (lost). They are the ones Jesus wants to reconnect with.

2. Children of God, our Creator, that are of the Kingdom of Heaven (found). They are the ones that have been "Reborn" or "Born Again".

It is obvious that our Creator is all about saving His Creation. The children of Adam, called the children of this world, are lost and in need of reconnection with their creator. Is there a specific location where these people live? Is there any specific language that these people use? There is one specific answer to these questions: Lost people live on earth. That is a no-brainer. Lost people live in darkness, and they promote lifestyles that revolve around darkness. Everyone who is separated from their Creator and controlled by their Egos is lost.

In Luke 18:11, the pharisee said, "I thank God I am not like that sinner". He believed he was better because of his behavior and not because of his connection. Jesus said that man was lost and would not be found. And the "sinner" (the guy the pharisee was so proud to be different from) was found because he realized he was lost.

So much of the challenge is in our mind and is controlled by our Ego. Ego judges the behavior (outward appearance), and God judges the heart of a person. Lost does not mean you are broke and not educated. In fact, it may be just the opposite. Wealthy and educated people may have the hardest time realizing that they are in a lost condition.

**Lost is a Connection Condition.**

This Connection Condition is the same for both types of people.

The first group of God's family just believes in the earthly world and in the Lust of the Flesh, the Lust of the Eyes, and the Pride of Life (LLP). Their Connection Condition is lost & connected to their Ego (world).

The second group is in the condition as the Lost. But they believe they need to be reborn into the Kingdom of Heaven. They used to live like the first group but now want to live by love, joy, and peace. For them, Connection Condition = Found and connected to their Creator

So, what is your Connection Condition = Lost or found?

The more we begin to look for lost people, the more people we find lost. Let's look at some of the ways we can reach these people. We see that a big group of people are lost because their leaders are educating and training them to live in a world of Lust of the Flesh, Lust of the Eyes and the Pride of Life (LLP). They are being kept in the dark about Jesus. In fact, they are being trained that these gods (lust of flesh, lust of eyes, and pride) are the way to a better life.

But even nature does NOT support this teaching. The National Geographic Institute did a study on 10 acres of the jungle. This study was being done to understand the survival of vegetation. So, they measured every tree 1 inch in diameter and greater. Then they came back each year to see the results. What they found was NOT what they expected. They expected that the strongest trees would survive and grow. However, what they found was that the ones that responded best to light survived and grew.

Nature shows us that "light" is the difference between what grows and what dies. This example is so profound. Life responds to light! Remember, Jesus is the light of the world, and if we keep people in darkness, they will be lost and die. We need a strategy for bringing Light to people living in darkness. This strategy must be unique for this earthly environment.

So, how do you bring light to lost people that like to live in darkness? As we look at these lost people, we see they are divided into different groups.

The first group of lost people who just want to live in the LLP (Lust, Lust and Pride) world can be divided into three subgroups.

1. People who are lost and don't care. They love living in darkness.

2. People who think they are found but are really lost.

3. People that think they are "found" just without Jesus.

### Subgroup 1

"Lost" and don't care people just want to take the "Blue Pill" and get back inside their cocoon. These people will not be interested in listening to the good news until their life demands it. For these people, we will need to set up Connection Answer Groups—groups that answer questions when life demands an answer.

People will not be interested...until life demands it!

An example of an Answer Group would be a Cancer Support Group or a group for parents who lost their children unexpectedly. I am sure you get the picture. It is a place where they can go and get answers to their miseries. There are many places we can set up in anticipation of life's "donkey" events. These are the people who require a crisis in their life before they are interested in even looking for the light. That is why Jesus spent lots of time helping and healing people. We need to be prepared when these people are looking for answers. Their "donkey" experience is coming, and we need to be ready to help them. Maybe then they will accept our help and be chosen to be found.

### Subgroup 2

"Found" but really lost people suffer from thinking that a person who is once found will continue to stay found so they can do anything they want. Paul tells us, "Those who endure to the end will be saved(found)." Adam was perfect and the son of God, yet he got lost!

These people don't realize that a new heart is a condition for being found. This "new heart" comes from dying "daily" to the flesh (LLP). Yes, dying daily to our ego. This means that we must choose to be "found" each day of our lives. You cannot just choose once. It's like telling someone you love them only once. But the "donkey" is coming, and what will they do when it comes? They still must realize that Jesus is the answer and not themselves.

Dying daily to our ego is a way of life.

As light comes into our lives, we see more of our earthly (fleshly) life in us. We may think that we have chosen Jesus for our salvation, but we have not chosen Jesus when it comes to leaving something we are attached to and choosing Jesus over it. Of course, it does not have to be skiing if you don't like to ski. That was one of my Ego attachments. Your Ego will keep reaching into your life, trying to keep darkness somewhere in your heart.

This daily battle is why it is necessary to be found again and again. Our flesh, our ego, keeps finding new ways to keep us from connecting 100% with our Creator. Our flesh and ego don't care what behavior it finds. It just does not want to "give up" control in our lives. Submitting all of our will and heart to Jesus is the condition connection to being found and staying found.

Yes, you can be found daily. That is the promise of Jesus when He said, 'I will send the Holy Spirit to help you to "die daily"'. Here are some ways to help people realize they are lost after their "donkey" experience.

Jesus says in Mark: "Listen! Behold, a sower went out to sow. And as he sowed, some seed fell along the path, and the birds came and devoured it. Other seed fell on rocky ground, where it did not have much soil, and immediately, it sprang up, since it had no depth of soil. And when the sun rose, it was scorched, and since it had no root, it withered away. Other seed fell among thorns, and the thorns grew up and choked it, and it yielded no grain. And other seeds fell into good soil and produced grain, growing up and increasing and yielding thirtyfold and sixtyfold and a hundredfold." And he said, "He who has ears to hear, let him hear." 4:3–9 (ESV)

**Subgroup 3**

People that think they are "found" without Jesus, here is an explanation about these people by Jesus.

"And when he was alone, those around him with the twelve asked him about the parables. And he said to them, 'you have been given the secret of the kingdom of God, but for those outside ("LOST") everything is in parable, so that they may indeed see but not perceive (they are lost), and may indeed hear but not understand, lest they should turn and be forgiven.'" These are the people that are destined to be lost. Please do not be one of them!

And then Jesus said to them, "Do you not understand this parable? The sower sows the word. (That is the Good News of how Jesus solved the 2 spiritual challenges that Satan brought against God.) And these are the ones along the path, where the word is sown: when they hear (the Good News), Satan immediately comes and takes away the word that is sown in them.

And these are the ones sown on rocky ground: the ones who, when they hear the word, immediately receive it with joy. And they have no root in themselves, but endure for a while; then, when tribulation or persecution arises on account of the word, immediately they fall away. And others are the ones sown among thorns. They are those who hear the word, but the cares of the world and the deceitfulness of riches and the desires for other things enter in and choke the word, and it proves unfruitful.

"Those that were sown on the good soil (God's children that He wants to save) are the ones who hear the word and accept it and bear fruit, thirtyfold and sixtyfold and a hundredfold." Mark 4:10–20.

Let's unpack this story of Jesus.

**Path People:**

The first group of people Jesus is talking about are the Path People. These people are the type of people that hear the word Jesus and are excited, but they want an easy path.

When the path calls for some commitment, they just want things their own way. The way of Jesus seems tough to them. They just turn to the 3 earthly gods (LLP). The Word Jesus is just plucked out of their lives.

**Rocky Ground People:**

The next group of people Jesus is talking about are the Rocky Ground People. These people are like the first group. They are also excited when they hear the Good News, but they don't see the need to change their lives. They believe their lives are good the way it is. However, when tough times come along, they blame God and stop believing. They thought that the Good News was a "Santa Gospel". God is someone with a bag full of toys. And when they find out God is much more than a bag of toys, they say, "See you later".

**Thorny Ground People:**

The last lost group of people that Jesus is talking about are the "Thorns People". These people are all about pretending they are God's children. They are really good at showing everyone that they are "holy". They are good people, and they want everyone to know just how good they are. This is the most blind group of all. We call these people "fair weather" Christians. They will sing in church, pray in church, give to missions as long as the thorns of life are not too bad.

# LOST AND FOUND

What are Thorns of Life, you ask? Jesus says they are the cares of this world. Now this does not sound bad. It's like caring about my job, my town, my country, and my family, but when these cares become more important than Jesus, we choke. Jesus also calls thorns the deceitfulness of riches. This is a slow death, just like boiling a frog.

I was sitting next to a former IRS agent who had just retired from managing 20,000 people. We were talking about value-based decisions message I heard from Dr. John Maxwell. He said, "I have seen many good people that just let money corrupt their entire life. Just one little cheat on their taxes that led to the next and the next and then to financial ruin. Focusing on getting rich is an illusion. You cannot chase riches!"

The last thorn Jesus talked about is possibly the most dangerous. Jesus calls "the desires for other things" thorn. Wow! This covers a whole bunch of stuff. We could say these desires are good because a person has desires. Desire for a spouse, children, new job, new trip, new adventure. Desire is so very deceptive because you think these desires are all good, but they get you lost. You might ask, "How are these causing me to be lost? I just have a healthy desire for baseball, cooking, skiing, or dancing?" But Jesus says these desires will take away your focus on heavenly activities. Good things can lead to a Lost Life. Even this type of people, according to Jesus, are NOT supposed to understand this parable!

As we look at the Found People, we see they also fit into three different groups.

**Good Soil People:**

The final group of people Jesus talks about are those who are children of Good Soil. These are the ones that have heard the Good News and have surrendered their egos to their Creator. They realized that life without Jesus was just a walking dead life. Jesus said, if you are not connected to your Creator, you do not have Eternal Life. Jesus goes beyond grouping all the Good Soil people in one group.

He divides them into 3 groups. Each group adds value as they grow from hearing the Word that Jesus said was the 'seed'. Seed = The Good News of the Gift of Jesus. The first group yields 30% fruit. They endorse the Message of Jesus victory and gift. Maybe they were found later in life and are doing all they can with what they have. They are using all their talents to help people to be found.

The next of the good soil people yield 60%. Maybe they were found earlier in life. Maybe they have more faith experiences and have many ways to share the Message. Their life is just more effective as they have been working for Jesus longer. They are also using all of their talents to share the Victory Message of Jesus.

The last of the good soil people yield 100%. In the parable, this person brings many people to Jesus. Even from a small child, their lives reflect Jesus. What a privilege they must have. What an example they are showing. All three groups are yielding all the fruit that they have. All are "all in" on Jesus. The sooner we are found, the sooner we can get to work on Challenge 3. Working with the Holy Spirit to find lost people!

# Chapter 23
# So What Do We Do Now?

Let's review the state of the world again. Most of God's people in this world are in a lost condition. Jesus said, "He came to seek and save those that were lost". Luke 19:10. Here, Jesus is talking about His lost children. That implies that not all people are God's children. In Matthew 13: 24-30, Jesus asked His disciples to leave the wheat and the tares growing together until the harvest. This comment of Jesus is very interesting as it tells us that the people that are "lovers of this world" will be allowed to be among His children until the time of the judgment. That means that all three groups will be found together until the end; God's lost children, God's found children and the world people—all will be living together until the end.

So, where does that leave us? Again, most of God's children were or are still lost, thanks to Adam. They need to find their way back to their Creator and the Kingdom of Heaven. Looking deeper at the parable of the Wheat and the Tares, we see an interesting picture. I believe a review of this story will show us two different important world views about the "Seed" people. And as we look at the words of Jesus, we will see that there are a whole lot of people in this world that will not be found. Simply put, they do not want to be found or they want to remain the people of the world. They want to live separated from God and live by their selfish ego.

This fact is revealed in several places in the Bible, starting from Genesis 6:1-4, where the Hebrew worldview tells us about the "sons of God", who came down and had sex with the daughters of man. Adam was a son of God, but Cain, Abel, and all of Adam's offspring were and are sons of man. This text shows us that the sons of God came down (from Heaven) to earth. They gave up their place in Heaven and created offspring in this world called Giants of the land. Giants is a translation that was used to describe someone that did NOT have Adam's complete DNA.

Again, Jesus shed some light on this subject when He answered the question about marriage in Heaven. Matthew 22:30. He said they will be like angels (they do not marry). Heaven had a different "condition" than the earth. They did not need or could not "connect" with each other as that was not the purpose in Heaven. I believe that the goal of the earth was to replace the $1/3^{rd}$ or more of Heaven's beings who chose to follow Lucifer. Marriage was and is an "Earth" privilege.

However, the fallen heavenly beings did NOT like their different "condition" being different than Earth People. So, they came down and partook of the beautiful earthly women. This was a major violation of God's will. Lucifer's goal was to dilute the DNA of God's children. He wanted to contaminate and then eliminate all of God's children and overthrow His Creation. His goal was to hurt God as he desired to be like Him. So, he thought he would create his own race by morphing God's DNA into his followers' DNA.

This was and is the agenda (message) of Satan, Mr. Ego to create a race of people after his kind, people who served their own ego and wanted to be their own gods. Satan did not tell them that the ego they all served was controlled by him. This race continued to grow and became more and more evil. When this race of people started to indulge in sexual perversions, God had to send the flood that wiped out the entire human race; well, all the people on earth except Noah and his family. Still, This hybrid race did not quit with the flood. It is still with us today.

It says in Genesis 6:4 that they were after the flood as well. We learn that in Numbers, 13:33, Joshua 11:21-22, Deuteronomy 3:11 and 1 Samuel chapter 17, all talk about this Nephilim race of people. Even today, there are movements to change and alter Adam's DNA. Let's look in Daniel to see if these people will be here till the end of time. Just like Jesus said, the "wheat and the tares" are together until the end.

We are given a clue in Daniel chapter 2:41-44 that the "clay" was people other than the "seed of men". [41] And as you saw the feet and toes, partly of [baked] clay [of the potter] and partly of iron, it shall be a divided kingdom; but there shall be in it some of the firmness *and* strength of iron, just as you saw the iron mixed with miry [earthen] clay.

⁴² And as the toes of the feet were partly of iron and partly of [dusty] clay, so the kingdom shall be partly strong and partly brittle *and* broken. A divided world. Sounds just like today.

⁴³ And as you saw the iron mixed with miry [burnt ash] *and* earthen clay, so they shall **mingle themselves** (who is Daniel talking about?) **in** the seed of men [these beings were having sex with humans]; but they will not hold together [for two such elements can never harmonize], even as iron does not mingle itself with clay.

⁴⁴ And in the days of these [final ten] kings shall the God of heaven set up His kingdom which shall never be destroyed, nor shall its sovereignty be left to another people; but it shall break *and* crush and consume all these kingdoms and it shall stand forever.

We see that there is going to be these "sons of the Nephilim" up to the final judgment and till the return of Jesus. Jesus also gave us a clue in Matthew 24 that what was going on at the time of the flood would also be happening at the end time.³⁷

As were the days of Noah, so will be the coming of the Son of Man.³⁸ For just as in those days before the flood they were eating and drinking, [men] marrying and [women] being given in marriage, until the [very] day when Noah went into the ark, ³⁹ And they did not know *or* understand until the flood came and swept them all away—so will be the coming of the Son of Man.

But Jesus gives us a promise in verse 31 when He says:

³¹ And He will send out His angels with a loud trumpet call, and they will gather His elect (His chosen ones) from the four winds, [even] from one end of the [j]universe to the other.

Paul also speaks in 1 Corinthians 15:52 "In a moment, in the twinkling of an eye, at [the sound of] the last trumpet call. For a trumpet will sound, and the dead [who believed in Christ] will be raised imperishable, and we will be [completely] changed [wondrously transformed]."

Trumpets are judgments in the Bible. In Daniel 2, we see that God's Kingdom smashed the image at the feet mixed with iron and clay and the whole image falls apart. This image represents the kingdom of this world. And the Rock cut out without hands is the Kingdom of Heaven. Jesus returns, the world is destroyed, and His Kingdom is set up!

In Revelation chapters 8, 9 and 11, we learn of the last 7 Trumpets or Judgments of God. In fact, Revelation 11:15 says: The seventh angel then blew [his] trumpet, and there were mighty voices in heaven, shouting, the dominion (kingdom, sovereignty, rule) of this (our) world, which has now come into the possession (of) and became the kingdom of our Lord and of His Christ (Jesus the Messiah), and He shall reign forever and ever (for the eternities of the eternities)!

What we have learned is that there is going to be a lot of people (the race of the Nephilim) living on the earth at the time of the last judgment of God and at the time of Jesus's return. There is a parable or story from Jesus that explains just what is going to happen. The story that we talked about in the last chapter is called: The Parable of the Wheat and the Tares. Matthew 13:24-30

²⁴ Another parable He put forth to them, saying: "The **kingdom of heaven** is like a man who sowed good seed (Good News that reconnect people to their Creator) in his field (our physical world) ²⁵ but while men slept, his enemy came and sowed tares (Satan's message) among the wheat and went his way. ²⁶ But when the grain had sprouted and produced a crop, then the tares also appeared. ²⁷ So the servants of the owner came and said to him, 'Sir, did you not sow good seed in your field? How then does it have tares?'

²⁸ He said to them, 'An enemy (Satan) has done this.' The servants said to him, 'Do you want us then to go and gather them up?' ²⁹ But he (God) said, 'No, lest while you gather up the tares you also uproot the wheat with them. ³⁰ Let both grow together until the harvest (the judgment), and at the time of harvest I will say to the reapers, "First gather together the tares and bind them in bundles to burn them, but gather the wheat into my barn."

The message is very subtle. Jesus starts with the words "The Kingdom of Heaven". He is talking about people who want to find the Kingdom of Heaven. However, we know that some of the people are not God's children. They have had their DNA altered. They are not interested in finding anything other than what pleases their ego (LLP). Just like people during the time of Noah, they are pursuing every pleasure and sexual desire they want.

This race of the Nephilim is taking God's creation and transforming human bodies into a "superior race" by any means. Transhumanism is enhancing the DNA of humans by artificial means, which dilutes the God-given DNA.

DNA modifications and vaccines to improve the body may appear to be progress, but nevertheless, it is changing our DNA. That leaves us with two races; one is the Children of God (God's DNA, and the other is the Children of this World (Satan's DNA). To be saved, both races must choose to be born again.

Jesus knows something about the Kingdom of Heaven and both races (wheat and tares). Jesus' gift covers both races if they choose. He knows which of His children want to find the Kingdom of Heaven. **Our mission**, if we choose to accept, is to "spread the good seed" to everyone because we do not know who is "Wheat and who is Tares". All the people of this physical world need to be shown that there is a Heavenly Kingdom. They need the "good seed" that Jesus is talking about to take root in their lives.

# LOST AND FOUND

*Jesus's gift of Eternal Life covers all types of lost people*

The comment in Matthew 13:35, "but while men slept", Jesus is showing that there is going to be a delay (to make sure no one is lost that should be found) in His return and the judgment. This delay is going to be an opportunity for Satan to spread the "bad seed". In fact, Jesus is saying that this bad seed is going to be around until the judgment.

Here is the rub. What is bad seed and what is good seed? And who is going to perceive the difference in the seeds and who will not? As Jesus said, "they may indeed see but not perceive (they are lost), and may indeed hear but not understand, lest they should turn and be forgiven." So, this story is about what soil you are.

God's people are going to get the "seed" they need to be reconnected with their Creator. They need to find the Kingdom of Heaven. The earthly world has their soil running their lives, and this is causing people to reject the Good News of Jesus. So, how do we tell people about their Connection (soil) Condition?

Remember the "good soil people". Who spreads (yield) the "seed" in the parable of the Sower? Is all the seed "good seed" in the parable? What is up with the good soil, people? What is up with the "path people"? In fact, the good seed is the same for all the people. But what happens to the seed when it falls on all types of soil? This is what I want to focus on in the rest of this chapter.

**Remember Good Soil People:**

But before we look at the 3 groups, let us look at the "soil". The good soil people grow food and produce "Fruits of the Spirit". This symbolizes that the "good soil" people feed good seed to "other people". All people will get either "good seed" or "bad seed".

What is the difference between "good seed" and "bad seed"? Jesus Victory Message is good seed. Lucifer's Ego Freedom Message is bad seed. If you have been a farmer, you will understand you do not want bad seed to be mixed with good seed. You will do whatever makes the soil more productive; soil preparation is the key. Depending on your preparation, your soil will produce a greater yield.

This is where Jesus makes his story very personal. Let us assume you and I are "good soil" people. What are you doing to prepare your soil? Are you tilling the soil enough to make it produce fruit? Tilling the soil is like studying God's Word. The Bible is the word of God that is designed to produce good fruit in each one of us. Are you spending enough time in God's word, tilling your heart?

There is more than just tilling, like watering the soil. Did you know that watering the soil not just helps the seeds grow but when the temperature drops to below freezing, watering the soil protects the plants and keeps them from freezing. The Bible calls it the shield of faith. We need protection to keep our hearts from freezing, for it does not take much for the heart to get cold.

And, of course, seeds do not grow without sunlight. Yes, without spending time in the presence of Jesus, we are not going to bear fruit. Jesus says there are 3 types of yields depending on how much time we spend with Jesus. The more time we are with Him, the more we become like Him. The Bible says it this way; By beholding Him, we become changed. The more fertile the soil, the more seeds will spring up and produce life in someone new.

We are responsible for our own soil. Jesus says, "that even if Job, Moses or Elijah were in the land (soil), they could only save themselves. Wow, even 3 of the greatest men on earth cannot bear fruit or food for anyone but for themselves. This story about the good soil is a very strong wake-up call for all of us who are "found". We better start working our own soil! But how do we prepare our own soil so we yield much fruit?

Let us start our search for answers with the words of Jesus in Matthew 5:44-46. $^{44}$But I say to you, love your enemies and pray for those who persecute you, $^{45}$so that you may be sons of your Father who is in heaven. For he makes the sun rise on the evil and on the good and sends rain on the just and on the unjust.$^{46}$For if you love those who love you, what reward do you have? Do not even the tax collectors do the same?

Does that mean we are to tell the good news to both the evil and good people? Yes, I think so. God, our Father, causes the sun and the rain to bless all people. Why? Because you do not know who is going to hear the Good News and respond. God knows his children, but we do not know. We do not know who is going to wake up and say Jesus, please save me in your Kingdom like the thief on the cross. So, even if we find out who is good and who is bad, it does not change who we share the Good News with! Remember, Jesus says let wheat and the tares remain together until the harvest.

Now that we are to tell the Good News to everyone, how should we share this news? Again, we can take our lead from Jesus. He focused on people that needed something. Usually, He started helping people who had physical needs. In fact, He would go to a town and heal everyone in the whole town. We see that it is important to help people physically because it gets their attention. If you cannot walk, talk, hear, or speak and then after meeting Jesus, you can, it should make it pretty easy to turn you into a believer.

"We love Him because Jesus first loved us"

Jesus does not stop at the physical world. He spent time with people to become their friend. He liked to visit people's homes for a meal. And He liked to go to celebration events. These events were where He could enjoy people's company and sometimes, He would help improve the event by adding to the food and drink. Jesus was very aware of people's daily needs. During the 3 ½ years Jesus spent sharing the news about His Kingdom of Heaven, He spent most of that time helping people in the physical world.

We talked about all of Jesus's miracles, and we saw that time after time, Jesus helped people before He spoke to them about His Kingdom and being found. But when Jesus did speak to the people about His Kingdom. He told them how to be born of the Spirit, how to surrender their ego to God, to seek first, the Kingdom of Heaven, and then He would supply the rest of our needs. Jesus did physical healing to earn people's trust, and then He showed them that He is the Way to His Heavenly Kingdom.

If we follow Jesus's example, then we need to first win the trust of people. This is one way we prepare our soil. I am reminded of the quote: "People do not care how much you know until they know how much you care". Jesus is showing time and time again that God, the Father, God, the Spirit and (God the Word) cares about their Creation. Yes, He cares. Just look back at the 2 of the 3 challenges of God and how Jesus answered and solved both challenges. He did this act of Love because we could not reconnect to our Creator ourselves.

Another way to prepare our soil is by following what Jesus said: "It is more blessed to give than to receive". He is showing us how to care for people. In the quantum world, we see the principle very clearly. It is called "the law of attraction". People are drawn to like frequencies because like attracts like. People are attracted to Jesus because of His Love frequencies. That is the frequency we need to be when we are sharing the Good News.

In 1 John 4:19, we are told that: "We love Him because Jesus first loved us". One good turn deserves another. This is the basic principle of sharing the Good News that Jesus is the Way to the Kingdom of Heaven. And remember, we are part of His solution in challenge #3. We are to share the Good News of God's Love! And the more soil prep we do, the greater the yield of our story will be.

There are many ways to show Love to people. Here is a short list to start with:

- Provide food
- Provide resources
- Provide education
- Provide healthcare
- Provide babysitting
- Provide transportation
- Provide training
- Provide support
- Provide company
- Provide direction
- Provide services

- Provide caring behaviors
- Providing acts of kindness
- Providing acts of joy

I know that this is just a short list, but it can give us a head start in earning people's trust. After we earn their trust, we can show them the way to the Heavenly Kingdom. How do you share the Way after you have earned people's trust? The Way comes from a guide. You cannot show the Way unless you have been there yourself. The Way back to God the Word (Jesus) involves sharing specific areas from our life. So, share your story with them.

**Humor**

We must share "our story" about Jesus and His Spirit; how they worked in our lives to bring us to the realization that we were Lost and then Found. Then tell them what happened to you after you Reconnected with our Creator. This story must be current, something people can relate to. Our story needs some humor, like how we can laugh at ourselves when we are in difficult spots. For example, the prodigal son when he was feeding pigs before he came to his senses. I am sure there was something about feeding pigs that was humorous.

**Drama**

Humor helps people relate to "our story". Drama is another part of our story that people relate to. For example, when I was driving home after a date, and I fell asleep at the wheel driving home. Yes, I crashed and was nearly killed. When the truck driver stopped to see if I was dead, and he saw me get out of the car, he nearly fainted. He and his daughter, who was with him, had watched the whole crash and assumed I was dead. When he saw me, he said that he believed God was watching over me that night! God works in mysterious ways!

**Science**

Science or facts is another part of our story. This part provides our listeners with confidence; we have truly been where we say we have been. There was a time when my wife Ilosha was visited by two angels. When she told me about it and what they were doing for her, I asked her one question:

What were the names of the angels? At that time, she did not know anything about the Bible and the names of angels in the Bible so if she knew the names of the angels, it meant her experience was real.

Yes, she had asked the angels their names: Michael and Raphael. We were on the phone when she told me this, and I dropped the phone as I could hardly believe she knew both of their names. Angels, Michael and Raphael, are angels and they have a part in Jesus's salvation solution. This knowledge helped me accept that her story was very real. Having said that, we don't need to prove our story as it is our story, but facts do play a part in our story.

## LOST AND FOUND

Again, our mission is to share our story of how we got found! We want all of God's children to be found! We know that Jesus will come when all of His children have chosen the Kingdom of Heaven as their new home! What do you think our new home will look like? Will it have a physical component? Is our new home our new immortal body? Will there be happiness and joy in our new home? Let's take a look at what Jesus says about His Kingdom of Heaven.

# Chapter 24
# The Lost Kingdom of Heaven

The Kingdom of Heaven is mentioned 33 times in the King James version of the Bible. This is a very important fact because Jesus is promising His lost children to reconnect (to be reborn) with Him (If they choose it). We have seen all the earthly reasons why we should want to reconnect, and now Jesus is promising us citizenship in the Kingdom of Heaven as a reward for our choice.

Let's look at some attributes of the Lost Kingdom of Heaven. This Kingdom has a few names: Lost Paradise, Garden of God, and God's home on earth. It was and is a place where our Creator can live in continual communication with His children. So, before He made Adam and Eve, God made a very beautiful and peaceful place for them to live, "The Garden of Eden". This tells us something very important about God! Where we live and how we live is important to God our Father, and our happiness and joy are requisite to our Creator.

Our first home, as humans, was the "Garden of Eden". This garden was perfect, and yet it was designed for growth and development. It had all the features of warmth and comfort. There were areas for each of the activities we would want to do to make us happy and to be in a relationship with our Creator. God wanted Adam and Eve to be in a home which was convenient for Him to visit. Imagine a home and garden built to entertain God and His angels. There are many houses designed with entertainment in mind, but who you entertain is the real question.

God wanted Adam and Eve to be in a home where it would be convenient for Him to visit. However, when Adam and Eve chose to separate from their Creator, they lost their home. Just like today, when you do not make your house payments, you lose your home. God's only required mortgage payment was to follow His direction and stay in a relationship with Him. But Adam and Eve missed their "mortgage" payments, and God had to foreclose (remove) them from their beautiful home and garden.

God, our Father, wants to reconnect and restore His children to Him and give each of us a new home! He loved the Garden and wanted to reconnect with His children and make them a new garden! There are more than 100 comments from our Creator to help us learn what His home and garden in The Kingdom of Heaven is going to be like. This Spiritual Kingdom of Heaven is going to restore peace, safety, and love for us all.

This is great news! In fact, this news alone should cause us to want to reconnect to our Creator. However, the battle for our choice is very real. Satan does not want to lose his claims (#1 and #2) regarding our Creator. Consider the fact that Lucifer no longer has eternal life. So, to live, he has to "eat" or "devour" food. Guess what? You are his food source! Possessing humans and their life energy is the only way he and his team continues to survive.

Peter tells us to: Be well balanced (temperate, sober of mind), be vigilant and cautious at all times; for that enemy of yours, the devil, roams around like a lion roaring [a][in fierce hunger], seeking someone to seize upon and devour. I Peter 5:8

You probably did not see yourself as food for Satan and his team. But since he lost his claims on Jesus, he will do his best to destroy (consume) God's creations. Jesus's mission and ours is to join and not let this happen! I do not want to be food for Satan. We must expose his purpose to destroy us. We must expose this deception and show God's lost children (and maybe even you) how they can reconnect and gain entrance to the Lost Kingdom of God. That is why Jesus said in Matthew 6:33: "But seek ye first the Kingdom of God, and his righteousness, and all these things shall be added unto you". He is, again, promising you citizenship in His Kingdom.

Now let's look at the definition of the phrase "Kingdom of Heaven". The word Kingdom speaks to the rule and governance of the Godhead over all things. The Bible speaks of this Kingdom existing in the past (Daniel 4:17, 25, 34, 5:21) [25] You will be driven away from people and will live with the wild animals; you will eat grass like the ox and be drenched with the dew of heaven. Seven times will pass by for you until you acknowledge that the most high is sovereign over all kingdoms on earth and gives them to anyone he wishes. [26] The command to leave the stump of the tree with its roots means that your kingdom will be restored to you when you acknowledge that "Heaven rules".

And then in Matthew 12:28 "But if it is by the Spirit of God that I drive out demons, then the kingdom of God has come upon you", Luke 17:20 – 21 "[20] Once, on being asked by the Pharisees when the kingdom of God would come", Jesus replied, "The coming of the kingdom of God is not something that can be observed, [21] nor will people say, 'Here it is,' or 'There it is,' because the kingdom of God is in your midst". Here is an awesome clue, The Kingdom of God must be experienced and NOT seen. In Colossians 1:13, "[13] For he has rescued us from the dominion of darkness and brought us into the kingdom of His Son ..." Jesus is the Kingdom! Another reason Jesus is the ONLY WAY to the kingdom. Again, God the Word became flesh and lived with us!

And then we find in Daniel 2:44, "In the time of those kings, the God of heaven will set up a kingdom that will never be destroyed, nor will it be left to another people. It will crush all those kingdoms and bring them to an end, but it will itself endure forever", 7:13 – 14 "In my vision at night I looked, and there before me was one like a son of man (Jesus), coming with the clouds of heaven. He approached the Ancient of Days and was led into his presence. [14] He was given authority, glory, and sovereign power; all nations and peoples of every language worshiped him. His dominion is an everlasting dominion that will not pass away, and his kingdom is one that will never be destroyed."

And in Revelation 11:15 – 18, "The kingdom of the world has become the kingdom of our Lord and of his Messiah, and he will reign for ever and ever."

21:1 "[21]Then I saw "a new heaven and a new earth,"[a] for the first heaven and the first earth had passed away, and there was no longer any sea" and finally, in Revelation 22:5, "There will be no more night. They will not need the light of a lamp or the light of the sun, for the Lord God will give them light. And they will reign for ever and ever."

*The Kingdom of God must be experienced and NOT seen.*

This invisible Kingdom has always existed because God has always existed. How do we know that? Because energy cannot be created or destroyed. God is Energy. He is the source of all life, the Consciousness of Life. Now since His Kingdom cannot be observed, then what defines His Kingdom? How do we experience this Kingdom? And when, if ever, does this Kingdom become both a Spiritual and Physical Kingdom? If we are going to become part of this Kingdom, answers to these questions would be helpful.

In our world, energy is the juice of life, and Consciousness cannot be conscious without Spirit. This is invisible to us in our World. We can feel it and experience it, but we cannot see it. (Energy and the Spirit). This is a simple example of how the Kingdom of Heaven and of God cannot be seen, but it is very real. This fit with Jesus's comments that "without faith it is impossible to please God". God desired a Spiritual (or Heart) Connection Condition with His Children.

It was explained by Jesus in His midnight meeting with Nicodemus in John 3:1-21 "Jesus answered, "I tell you the solemn truth, unless a person is born of water and spirit, he cannot enter the kingdom of God. 6What is born of the flesh is flesh, and what is born of the Spirit is spirit. 7Do not be amazed that I said to you, 'You must be born from above.' 8The wind blows wherever it wishes, and you hear the sound of it, but do not know where it comes from and where it is going. So, it is with everyone who is born of the Spirit."

*"The Kingdom of Heaven is at hand."*

God's Kingdom started for Adam and Eve with a combination of both Spiritual and Physical dimensions but when they disconnected from their Creator, they lost Spiritual Connection. God's Kingdom then split apart. We were left with "the kingdom of this world" Revelation 15:11 and we learned that without Jesus the Word, we had no way back to the Kingdom of Heaven. That leaves us now with the Lost Kingdom of Heaven. This Lost Kingdom is now the

Spiritual Kingdom that Jesus was talking about when He was here on this earth. He is talking about what Adam and Eve (and us) lost in the Garden Event.

And until He returns, we need to focus on reconnecting with this Spiritual Kingdom. That is why Jesus said that the Kingdom of Heaven is now. The Kingdom of Heaven can be found! "The time is fulfilled, and the kingdom of God is at hand; repent and believe in the gospel."—Mark 1:15. The Kingdom of Heaven drew near to us when God himself came to earth in the form of Jesus. This is what is meant by John when he said, "The Kingdom of Heaven is at hand." He tells us that the Kingdom of Heaven is now available today through the Person of the King Jesus!

Repent for following your selfish ego and reconnect with your Creator. This is the first step in finding the Lost Kingdom of Heaven. Now there is even GREATER news; Jesus is going to reunite both, the Spiritual and Physical Kingdoms of God when He returns! First, He is going to give us new physical bodies so we can live in the Spiritual World. He will make our earthly home (body) immortal and by then, our Spiritual Body will have already been reborn. Now it is our Creator's desire to combine both the physical world and the spiritual world into our Garden, called the Kingdom of Heaven.

We are given several pictures and descriptions of what that new Home and Garden (Kingdom of Heaven) will look like. Let's take a look at some of those references. Peter gives us God's promise in 2 Peter 3:13, "[13] But according to His promise, we are looking for new heavens and a new earth, in which righteousness dwells." This is a beautiful combination of both the Spiritual and the Physical worlds.

Isaiah 65, "See, I will create new heavens and a new earth. The former things will not be remembered, nor will they come to mind. [18] But be glad and rejoice forever in what I will create, for I will create Jerusalem to be a delight and its people a joy. [19] I will rejoice over Jerusalem and take delight in my people; the sound of weeping and of crying will be heard in it no more. [20] "Never again will there be in it an infant who lives but a few days, or an old man who does not live out his years; the one who dies at a hundred will be thought a mere child; the one who fails to reach[a] a hundred will be considered accursed. [21] They will build houses and dwell in them; they will plant vineyards and eat their fruit. [22] No longer will they build houses and others live in them, or plant and others eat. For as the days of a tree, so will be the days of my people; my chosen ones will long enjoy the work of their hands. [23] They will not labor in vain, nor will they bear children doomed to misfortune; for they will be a people blessed by the Lord, they and their descendants with them. [24] Before they call I will answer; while they are still speaking I will hear. [25] The wolf and the lamb will feed together, and the lion will eat straw like the ox, and dust will be the serpent's food. They will neither harm nor destroy on all my holy mountain," says the Lord.

Our Creator is going to make a new "earthly" world and all the pain and suffering from this world will be forgotten. People and animals will be at peace with each other. God will encourage us to build new houses and plant some awesome vineyards. All of us will be safe and enjoy the fruits of our labor. And there will be no evil again! Thank you, Jesus!

Isaiah again says in chapter 66:22, "For just as the new heavens and the new earth *Which I make* will endure before Me," declares the Lord. We see God's promise that He is going to make a New Heaven and a New Earth that will endure forever. Matthew goes on to quote Jesus in chapter 5, verse 5, and says, "Blessed are the meek, for they shall inherit the earth. This is where Jesus in the Sermon on the Mount promises the meek and humble Children of God new earth!

Jesus says in John 14:1-3, "Do not let your heart be troubled; believe in God, believe also in Me. ² In My Father's house are many dwelling places; if it were not so, I would have told you; for I go to prepare a place for you. ³ If I go and prepare a place for you, I will come again and receive you Myself, that's where I am, *there* you may be also." Jesus is not only telling you and me that He is returning to redeem us from this world, but He is also preparing us a new Home and Garden for us to live with Him forever!

With all these promises, we also need to listen to Jesus when He says in Mark 13:31, "Heaven and earth will pass away, but My words will not pass away. He is giving us a

# LOST AND FOUND

heads-up that this physical heaven (sky) and earth are going to be destroyed. Since He created this world, He can destroy it as well.

In Matthew chapter 25:31- 46, He tells us what would happen if you are and if you are not reconnected to Him, [34] "Then the King will say to those on His right, 'Come, you who are blessed by My Father, inherit the Kingdom prepared for you from the foundation of the world.[46] These will go away to eternal punishment, but the righteous into eternal life."

But Jesus makes this promise in Matthew 5:18 when He says, "[18] For truly I say to you, until heaven and earth pass away, not the smallest letter or stroke shall pass from the Law until all is accomplished." Then He goes on to add, "[19] Whoever then 'makes void' one of the least of these commandments, and teaches others *to do* the same, shall be called least in the kingdom of heaven; but whoever keeps and teaches *them*, he shall be called great in the kingdom of heaven."

Again, Jesus is giving us clues about the Kingdom of Heaven. Both the Spiritual and Physical Kingdom(s).

God inspires John in Revelation chapter 21 to give us some more pictures of what His Kingdom of Heaven will look like. He says, "Then I saw a new heaven and a new earth; for the first heaven and the first earth passed away, and there is no longer *any* sea. [2] And I saw the holy city, new

Jerusalem, coming down out of heaven from God, made ready as a bride adorned for her husband. ³And I heard a loud voice from the throne, saying, 'Behold, the tabernacle of God is among men, and He will dwell among them, and they shall be His people, and God Himself will be among them, ⁴and He will wipe away every tear from their eyes, and there will no longer be *any* death; there will no longer be *any* mourning, or crying, or pain; the first things have passed away.' ⁶Then He said to me (John), 'It is done. I am the Alpha and the Omega, the beginning, and the end. I will give to the one who thirsts from the spring of the water of life without cost. ⁷He who overcomes will inherit these things, and I will be his God and he will be My son."

"⁵And He who sits on the throne said, 'Behold, I am making all things new.' And He said, 'Write, for these words are faithful and true.'

This sounds very physical as Jesus is showing us just how awesome and beautiful our new home is going to be. Our Creator has promised to be our Father! No ifs, ands, or buts about it. God has fully reconnected with His Children.

Again, God promised to make a new combined and connected Physical and Spiritual Kingdom for His Children. He wants them to forget all the past physical world of pain and loss and live in a relationship with Him forever. Then Jesus adds to these promises some promises as to what He is going to do for us.

In Acts 1:11, He says, "They also said, 'Men of Galilee, why do you stand looking into [a]the sky? This Jesus, who has been taken up from you into heaven, will come in just the same way as you have watched Him go into heaven.'" Jesus is not leaving us here in this evil world.

Now that He is not leaving us here, He goes on to say in Colossians chapter 3, "Therefore if you have been raised with Christ, keep seeking the things above, where Christ is, seated at the right hand of God. ²Set your mind on the things above, not on the things that are on earth. ³For you have died and your life is hidden with Christ in God. ⁴When Christ, who is our life, is revealed, then you also will be revealed with Him in glory." Are you ready for this "glory"?

And again, in Philippians 3:21, we are told, "Jesus will transform our lowly body to be like his glorious body, by the power that enables him even to subject all things to himself." Yes, He is coming back to get us. He is making us new homes in Heaven and He is going to give us Immortal Bodies! I am telling you this is more than we can imagine.

And finally, He is inviting us to a Banquet Feast. He calls it the Wedding Supper of the Lamb (Jesus). Here is His personal invite to you: Luke 13:29 Jesus says, "²⁹And they will come from east and west and north and south, and will recline *at the table* in the Kingdom of God.

And just in case you did not hear Him in Luke chapter 13, Jesus will make sure you hear Him in Revelation 19:6-

9, "Then I heard what seemed to be the voice of a great multitude, like the roar of many waters and like the sound of mighty peals of thunder, crying out,"

"Hallelujah! For the Lord, our God the Almighty reigns. ⁷Let us rejoice and exult and give him the glory, for the marriage of the Lamb has come, and his Bride (that's us!) has made herself ready; ⁸it was granted her to clothe herself with fine linen, bright and pure"— for the fine linen are the righteous deeds (our deeds are accepting Jesus' gift) of the saints.

⁹And the angel said to me (John), "Write this: Blessed are those who are invited to the Marriage Supper of the Lamb." And he said to me, "These are the true words of God." Drop the mic!

What more is there to say?

1. Lay aside your Ego, and choose Jesus, God the Word, and His free gift.
2. Become a Child of God, our Creator.
3. Hold on to Jesus and get ready to go to a New Heaven and a New Earth!
4. I hope and pray I see you there my Friend.
5. Until then, spread the Good News.

LOST AND FOUND

**It is the end of the beginning!**

# Chapter 25
# Pascal's Wager

Please understand that I am sharing Pascal's writings from the position of "heart reason" of the soul. We must believe with the "heart", or we do not believe at all. Pascal believed in God as the Creator of Mathematics, Physics, and Reason. God says through Isaiah in chapter 1:18, "Come now, let us reason together, says the LORD; though your sins are like scarlet, they shall be as white as snow; though they are red like crimson, they shall become like wool.

For those of you who are "Bereans," I will try to provide you with some logic and reason to accept the call of our Creator. When I am done, I believe you will arrive at the conclusion to; "Be still and know that I am God". We suffer from living in our Flesh. This conditioned body and mind will cause us more pain and suffering than you can imagine. Our Creator has "sent us the Holy Spirit" to show us how to "live by the Spirit". I hope this "logic chapter" will help you.

Early in life, Blaise Pascal (1623-1662) pursued interests in physics and mathematics. His theory of conic sections and probability theory are well known; nevertheless, his experimental methodology in physics proved just as influential, especially his research in hydrostatics. His correspondence with Fermat helped establish the foundations of probability theory; his correspondence with Leibniz helped establish the foundations of calculus.[3]

Then because of a near-death accident, Pascal turned his attention to God and religious philosophy. It seems he was driving a four-in-hand team of horses when the two lead horses leaped over the parapet of Neuilly Bridge. Pascal's life was saved when the traces broke; Pascal took the accident as a sign to abandon his experimental life and turn to God. For the remainder of his life, he carried a piece of parchment describing this incident next to his heart.

Here is the argument for God by Pascal.

**That God Is**

"We know that there is an infinite and we are ignorant of its nature. As we know it to be false that numbers are finite, it is, therefore, true that there is an infinity in numbers. But we do not know what it is. It is false that it is *even*, it is false that it is *odd*; for the addition of a unit can make no change in its nature. Yet it is a number, and every number is odd or even this is certainly true of every finite number.

So, we may well know that there is a God without knowing what He is. Is there, not one substantial truth,

---

[3] Pascal, B. (1910). The wager. Philosophy of Religion.

seeing that there are so many things which are not the truth itself?

We know the existence and nature of the finite because we also are finite and have an extension. We know the existence of the infinite and are ignorant of its nature because it has extensions like us, but not limits like us. But we know neither the existence nor the nature of God because He has neither extension nor limits.

But by faith, we know His existence; in glory (Kingdom of Heaven) we shall know His nature. Now, I have already shown that we may well know the existence of a thing without knowing its nature.

Let us now speak according to natural lights. If there is a God, He is infinitely incomprehensible, since, has neither parts nor limits. He has no affinity with us. We are then incapable of knowing either what He is or if He is. This being so, who will dare to undertake the decision of the question? Not we, who have no affinity to Him.

Who then will blame Christians for not being able to give a reason for their belief since they profess a religion for which they cannot give a reason? (this is the reason that our Creator – God the Word – came in the human form as Jesus) They declare, in expounding it to the world, that it is foolishness, and then you complain that they do not prove it! If they proved it, they would not keep their words; it is in lacking proof, that they are not lacking in sense.

But although this excuses those who offer it as such and take away from them the blame of putting it forward without reason, it does not excuse those who receive it. Let us then examine this point, and say, "God is, or He is not" but to which side shall we incline? Reason can decide nothing here.

There is an infinite chaos that separates us. A game is being played at the extremity of this infinite distance where heads or tails will turn up. What will you wager? (choose). According to reason, you can do neither do one thing nor the other; according to reason, you can defend neither of the propositions.

Do not then reprove (judge) for error those who have made a choice; for you know nothing about it. "No, but I blame them for having made, not this choice, but a choice; for again both he who chooses heads and he who chooses tails are equally at fault; they are both in the wrong. The true course is not to wager at all. (but when you do not wager you do not live at all)

**"The Wager"**

—Yes; but you must wager (choose). It is not optional. (You are Conscious.) Which will you choose then? Let us see. Since you must choose, let us see which interests you least. You have two things to lose, the true and the good; and two things to stake, your reason and your will, your knowledge, and your happiness; and your nature has two things to shun, error and misery. Your reason is no more shocked in choosing one rather than the other since you must of necessity choose.

This is one point settled. But your happiness? Let us weigh the gain and the loss in wagering that God is. Let us estimate these two chances. If you gain, you gain all; if you lose, you lose nothing. Wager them without hesitation that He is. "That is very fine. Yes, I must wager; but I may perhaps wager too much."

—Let us see. Since there is an equal risk of gain and of loss, if you had only to gain two lives instead of one, you might still wager. But if there were three lives to gain, you would have to play (since you are under the necessity of playing), and you would be imprudent when you are forced to play, not to chance your life to gain three at a game where there is an equal risk of loss and gain. But there is an eternity of life and happiness.

And this being so, if there were an infinity of chances, which one only would be for you? You would still be right in wagering one to win two. You would act stupidly, being obliged to play. (Why?) Because by refusing to stake one life (choices) against three at a game in which out of an infinity of chances there is one for you if there were an infinity of an infinitely happy life to gain (all could be lost).

But there is an infinity of an infinitely happy life to gain, a chance of gain against a finite number of chances of loss.

And what you stake is finite. It is all divided; wherever the infinite is and there is not an infinity of chances of loss against that of gain. There is no time to hesitate, you must give all. And thus, when one is forced to play, he must renounce reason to preserve his life, rather than risk it for infinite gain, as likely to happen as the loss of nothingness.

For it is no use to say it is uncertain if we will gain, and it is certain that we risk, and that the infinite distance between the certainty of what is staked and the uncertainty of what will be gained, equals the finite good which is certainly staked against the uncertain infinite. It is not so, as every player stakes a certainty to gain an uncertainty, and yet he stakes a finite certainty to gain a finite uncertainty, without transgressing against reason.

There is not an infinite distance between the certainty staked and the uncertainty of the gain; that is untrue. In truth, there is an infinity between the certainty of gain and the certainty of loss. But the uncertainty of the gain is proportioned to the certainty of the stake according to the proportion of the chances of gain and loss.

Hence it means; if there are as many risks on one side as on the other, the course is to play even; and then the certainty of the stake is equal to the uncertainty of the gain. So far it is from the fact that there is an infinite distance between them. And so, our proposition is of infinite force, when there is the finite to stake in a game where there are equal risks of gain and loss, and the infinite to gain.

This is demonstrable; and if men are capable of any truths, this is one. "I confess it, I admit it. But still is there no means of seeing the faces of the cards?"—Yes, Scripture and the rest, &c.—"Yes, but I have my hands tied and my mouth closed; I am forced to wager, and am not free. I am not released and am so made that I cannot believe. What then would you have me do?"

Read the above lines as many times as you need to so you can understand what he is saying.

**The Heart Has Its Reasons**

True. But at least learn your inability to believe since reason brings you to this, and you cannot believe. Endeavor then to convince yourself, not by increase of proofs of God, but by the abatement of your passions. You would like to attain faith and do not know the way; you would like to cure yourself of unbelief and ask the remedy for it. Learn of those who have been bound like you, and who now stake all their possessions. These are people who know the way which you would follow and who are cured of an ill of which you would be cured.

Follow the way by which they began; by acting as if they believe, taking the holy water, having church said, &c. Even this will naturally make you believe, and deaden your acuteness.—"But this is what I am afraid of"—And why? What have you to lose?

But to show you that this leads you there, it is this which will lessen the passions, which are your stumbling blocks.

The heart has its reasons which reason does not know. We feel it in a thousand things. I say that the heart naturally loves the Universal Being (God our Creator), and also itself naturally, according as it gives itself to them; and it hardens itself against one or the other at its will. You have rejected the one and kept the other. Is it by reason that you love yourself?

It is the heart that experiences God and not the reason. This, then, is faith; God felt by the heart, not by reason.

Yes, this "Wager" demands a very clear mind to understand. Some would say that Pascal's arguments for God are very complex and difficult. But he is trying to say that you have nothing to lose by believing in God our Creator because you stake your all in your choice. The downside of believing in God is that you lose your passions which causes you pain and unhappiness. The upside is to know God and receive happiness and joy. You receive an Awesome Eternity! Either way, you stake it all by your decision.

*Thank You, Pascal*

# Epilogue
# Welcome to the Lost Kingdom of Heaven

Why do I know about this Kingdom of Heaven? Because Jesus, God the Word, is real to me. I have experienced Jesus. And in moments when I experienced the Kingdom of Heaven, He spoke to me. I will spend a few moments sharing with you some of those moments. My goal in this is to show you that there is more than "random chance" that works in your life. I don't know why we spend our whole life explaining everything away as "random chance"? Why do we refuse to choose when by not choosing, you stake it all on random chance?

I am reminded of the story of the roofer that was on a very steep roof. He began to slide down the roof, and he cried out, "Jesus save me"! Just then, his pants caught on a nail that what sticking up. His response was, "Never mind Jesus, I got this myself." We smile, and yet we do the same thing day after day. In our earthly ways, we love the thought that we are special. We think being blessed by random chance is cooler than being blessed by God, our Creator. Welcome to Las Vegas, the biggest game of chance. Now how dumb is that? Chance has no consciousness. Chance has no relationship with you. Random Chance is just Random Chance.

## LOST AND FOUND

When I was 5 years old, I used to pray to the "God" that I knew. Well, I thought I knew. You see, my biological father died when I was 2 years old, and I had no father to comfort me. I was a timid boy at that time and fighting was not in my nature. I loved to run, draw, play in the sand, and slide down our 12-foot slide. However, I was afraid of the dark. I could not even explain it to my mom or my grandparents.

So, what did I do? I did the only thing I thought would solve the problem. I prayed to "my Father in Heaven" to let me die; each night. Then I asked Him to wake me up from the dead each morning. This way, I would be dead during the night, and anything that happened I would miss. But just in case, I asked him to raise me from the dead each morning. Sounds silly now, doesn't it? But that was all I had at that time, and it was my way of dealing with fear.

The thought that God would do that for me through prayer gave me comfort. I felt He heard me and cared enough for me to listen and act. This is the belief I want you to see. I have learned in my studies of Quantum Physics that the Observer is the one that "collapses the wave function" and "defines reality." There is no "random chance" in our lives. Our "observation", our "faith", and our "Certainty" in Jesus are what make our reality.

I had my first "Angel" experience when I was in 3rd grade. My grandad had just built a new house for my mom and stepdad. We had lived in the house for about 2 months.

By the way, I still was somewhat afraid of the dark. My brother and I had bunk beds, and I slept on the top bunk. It may have been because I was the oldest and I had the first choice. Regardless, I was on the top bunk. I had just fallen asleep. The room was dark, and the door shut.

I was awoken by a bright light in the room. At first, I thought it was someone that had turned on the light, but it was not coming from the ceiling. I remember raising my head from the pillow and looking down toward my feet. I did not believe my eyes. An angel was standing by my bed. The angel was very big and bright orange/yellow. I could see his face and hands. The angel also had big, beautiful wings and was just watching over my brother's bed and my bed.

Another time when God took care of me was in high school. I was in 10$^{th}$ grade. This school was a boarding academy with pretty strict rules. On Thursday evenings, we had town night. We all looked forward to going to town. We could enjoy restaurant food, buy new clothes if we had the money or just hang out. We only had one rule, and that was to be on the bus at 8 pm when it leaves to go back to the dorm!

This was before there were cell phones or even pagers! Wow, that was a long time ago. Ugh. Needless to say, I missed the bus. I was a kid that did not want to break the rules and did not want to get suspended from school! Now, I was a good runner, so I started running back the 5 miles to school. I knew that there was NO WAY I was going to beat the bus back. So, I slowed down and started to pray. Just a simple prayer for God to help me get back to school on time.

Before I was able to say amen, my boss from the school dairy pulled up and said, "Jerry do you need a ride"? I was so amazed that I just looked at him for a couple of seconds before I said, YES! He said, "Jump in." In a few minutes, we passed the school bus and I made it back to school before the bus. I have never forgotten that experience. It is one of those times when you know God hears you.

One night when I was 17 years old, God heard my mother's prayer. He knew that I needed angels to watch over me that night. I needed extra protection driving home from Salem. I was a junior in high school. My girlfriend at that time had just broken up with me, and I was on a rebound date. I took Sharon to the Oregon State Fair for the evening. We stayed out too late. I was not a good time manager at that time, and I was going to have an hour's drive home to Portland.

After I dropped Sharon off at her home, I remember putting on my seatbelt and thinking *I should wear it.* By the way, I never wore my seatbelt in 1971. However, that night I buckled my seatbelt. That night I would have died without my seatbelt on! Driving home, I fell asleep at the wheel. The trucker that stopped after my accident said I passed him going more than 85 mph. I took out 100 feet of center guard rail before hitting the bridge. I hit it so hard that the engine split, and the impact sheared the wheels from the axle. The car stopped right before going through the outside guard rail and into the river below.

Praise Jesus, I was alive! My car was totaled. I got a ticket. But I was alive. I did have a few broken ribs. On my way to the hospital, I had time to realize that God watches out for us even when we make stupid decisions. And because God is our Creator, He used that experience to speak to the truck driver and his daughter that miracles do happen in 1971. They also became believers in Jesus.

Now for those of you who want a "current" answer to prayer, I will give you two.

Our company was impacted by the COVID flu virus, and our revenue was reduced by half from 2019 to 2020. Small Business Administration was offering some low-interest loans. We had taken advantage of some very small loan options but nothing that would really help us recover in a big way. So, we made an application for a larger amount of funding in July 2021. It had been over 60 days, and we had not heard anything.

In September, we were invited to a Friday night church service with a Masonic Rabbi giving the service. His service was divided into 2 parts. Part 1 was about Jesus as our savior and stories about His life. So far, praise Jesus. Part 2 was about how the Jews were still God's chosen people. We Gentiles just needed to realize that in the end times, right before the return of Jesus, the Jews were going to get special treatment. We Gentiles were NOT God's chosen people.

When my wife and I went on a walk later that evening, I was telling her that I did not agree that the Jews were any more God's favorite than the Gentiles. God views all people the same. And Paul said in Romans 10:12 that both Jew and Gentile were one in Jesus. Here are a couple of Paul's quotes.

[14] For He Himself is our peace, who made both *groups into* one and broke down the barrier of the dividing wall,

[15] by abolishing in His flesh the enmity, *which is* the Law of commandments *contained* in ordinances, so that in Himself He might make the two into one new man, *thus* establishing peace,

[16] and might reconcile them both in one body to God through the cross, [o]by it having put to death the enmity.

[17] And He came and preached peace to you who were far away, and peace to those who were near;

[18] for through Him we both have our access in one Spirit to the Father.

[19] So then you are no longer strangers and aliens, but you are fellow citizens with the [p]saints, and are of God's household," Ephesians 2:14-19

And as I was getting worked up while I was talking to my wife, I made a vow to God. PS: You might want to be careful making vows to God. Just saying! In hindsight, I could have been a little less worked up. But if you know me, that is not my style. So, I said to God in front of my wife that if God would put all the requested SBA loan monies in our bank account by Monday, then I would write a book on "The Lost and Found", God's clear plan for His Children.

Remember, I had not even received approval from the SBA, let alone any notice of funding. I felt pretty sure God was not listening and I would not actually write the book on the Lost and Found. But I was passionate about who God is inviting to the "Lost Kingdom of Heaven"? My wife was interested. She agreed with me that God's Children, "The Bride of Jesus", were both Jew and Gentile. She said, "Okay, Jerry, let's see what God does." We then wrote it on our calendar that Saturday night.

On Sunday afternoon, I received an email that all the money requested would be deposited in our bank on Monday! Some important facts to consider before you go to random chance.

1. SBA does not work on the Sunday.

2. It had been over 60 days since I had made an application with NO response.

3. 15 hours after I made that promise to God the monies were confirmed.

Obviously, I started writing the book! I began in earnest to write as I was excited for God's answer. I got the outline done and started on Chapter 1. I was making good progress until about chapter 8. Then with the new SBA monies in the bank, I started to pivot back to work and to get consumed by the life of this world. I started to put off writing. I was still making some progress, but it was very slow. Then along came November 9. The day God knocked me off my "donkey", so to speak. A little like He did to the Apostle Paul.

At 5:15 am on November 9, 2021, I felt a small electronic buzz at the top and a little right of center in my head. I lost my balance. Hum, that was weird. I went back to bed, and then my left side started to go numb. First my left hand, and then my left ear, then my left rib cage, then my left foot. My wife asked me what was wrong, and I said, "If I did not know better, I think I am having a stroke". We lay there for a few minutes, and then I decided to let her take me to the hospital.

She drove me to the hospital, and as we arrived in the waiting room of the emergency room, the nurse came out to us. She said, "You are outside the time for a "TPA" shot. Now I had never heard of a TPA shot, so I just said okay and proceeded to share the morning events. Upon verification of the stroke, they moved me to the Methodist trauma care hospital in Dallas. We arrived at the trauma hospital and went through the same testing and cat scan as before.

The devil always attacks you when you are down!

In the meantime, my wife just got a call from her dad's wife in Russia saying her dad had just died of myocarditis caused by the COVID vaccine he had just received 5 days earlier. Oh my God! Just imagine her husband is in the hospital with a stroke, and her dad just died, all on the same day. What were we to do? I was stuck in the hospital, and she needed to leave for Russia. To add to the confusion, the doctor walked into my room and said you have 10 minutes to decide. What decision?

I would be out of the "time window" in 10 minutes to receive the "TPA" shot. And if I got this shot of "TPA" within the next 10 minutes, it could reverse all the stroke symptoms. Wow! I did not know what to do. So, my wife and I prayed and asked Jesus to show us what to do. Then, I asked the doctor what the symptoms and risks were in getting this shot. He said that I had an 8% chance of bleeding out. Yes, 8% chance of dying. Then there were the words of the nurse from the first hospital, "You are outside the TPA window". I still did not understand. But my wife had just lost her dad, and I was going to give her an 8% chance of losing her husband too? No, I will trust Jesus!

My wife left for Russia, and I went in for more tests. After a whole bunch of tests, the doctor came back to my room and said that I had had a stroke and at least one more stroke earlier. Maybe as long as a month before. He also told me that the "TPA" shot would not have done anything because I had already had at least 1 stroke earlier. Now, remember that nurse back in the other hospital that said, "You are outside the time." Now I understood, God sent me a warning not to get the shot because it would be of no good. Well, not earthly good except give me an 8% chance of bleeding out.

God was watching out for both my wife and me. He wanted to spare her any more loss and trauma, and He wanted to save my life. Plus, He reminded me of my vow to Him to write the book. This is a very real relationship with Jesus that we both experienced. It felt like we were walking with Jesus in the "cool of the day". And now I am very motivated to finish this book! He gave us money to restart our business and He gave us warnings that saved our lives. Thank you, Jesus!

These are just a few of the miracles Jesus did in my life. Maybe someday I will write a book on God's miracles in my life. It will be a big book with lots of stories as I am 69 years old! There is not a day that goes by that Jesus and His Angels don't do something for my wife and me. It is a real relationship. I say, "Expect a miracle". It could be something like an impression to not hire a person. Or go to that store and meet someone that needs a word of encouragement. Help that person. Give that person some money. Pray with that person. He is trying to reach His children. Will you help Him?

Our communication with Jesus is similar to what Adam and Eve had in the Garden of Eden.[8] They heard the sound of the Lord God walking in the garden in the cool of the day" Genesis 3:8. Jesus, "the author of life", came and walked with them in the afternoon when lite breeze cooled off the day. He even walked with them when they chose to separate themselves from Him. That is a relationship!

I now live my life by the words of Jesus. "But seek ye first the kingdom of God, and his righteousness; and all these things shall (things that the people of the world seek) be added unto you." Matthew 6:33

We all must believe that Jesus is real and that He is the reward of those who seek Him. For, "without faith, it is impossible to please Him: for he that cometh to God (our Creator) must believe that He is and that He is a rewarder of them that diligently seek Him. Hebrews 11:6

I am reminded that when Jesus was here on earth, He would ask people, "What do you want"? See Mark 10:51, John 1:38, and Luke 18:41. This was Jesus's practice. And the person would say what they wanted to see, to walk, or to be healed. The person had to believe that Jesus was God our Creator and Healer, and He could help them. And then, when they would tell Jesus what they wanted, He would say, "Your Faith has healed you"!

## LOST AND FOUND

*I want to see Jesus!*

Faith in Jesus as your Creator released the healing energy in Jesus. Jesus released His healing energy. Just like the time when Jesus said, "Somebody hath touched me; for I perceive that virtue (healing energy) is gone out of me." Luke 8:46 The woman that touched Jesus's robe was so committed that she believes anything was possible. Jesus could change reality. She could be changed in a moment, in the blink of an eye, and be whole.

Do you believe that? Do you think God can change you in a moment and the blink of an eye? Or do you think that it is just a story, and Jesus does not heal today? Jesus is so interested in your life that He will do anything to get you to believe. Even leave the Kingdom of Heaven and take the form of a Human. And then die to pay the reconnection fee so you can "be found"!

Here is the path for you to find the Lost Kingdom of Heaven:

1. Realize you are lost and NOT in the Kingdom of Heaven!
2. Repent your lost choices!
3. Believe in Jesus as your Creator!
4. Believe that Jesus answered all the challenges of Satan

a. Live with "free will" in human flesh and always choose a connection with the Father

   b. Pay the reconnection fee by dying the "separation death" and getting the "keys of hell" for us.

   c. Living on this earth to "show us the way" to the Kingdom of Heaven"

5. Commit to a living relationship with Jesus

   a. Growth and change come after commitment

   i. Change does not come before commitment!

6. Learn to Resist Doubt

   a. If you doubt, we are told you are "damned"

   b. But when you ask God, you must believe [ask with faith] and not doubt. Anyone who doubts is like a wave in the sea, blown up and down [driven and tossed] by the wind. James 1:6

7. Enjoy the Certainty that comes from your commitment to please God by Faith in Jesus

In closing, my most recent vision was in May 2022. My wife and I were sleeping. I usually sleep on the right side. But in my vision, I was on the left side. Our bed was in a wheat field, and the weather was nice and warm. There were floating clouds in the sky when all of a sudden, these large stairs appeared in the clouds. The clouds parted, and the stairs floated down toward the earth.

## LOST AND FOUND

The stairs were very clear, and the steps were grey with golden handrails. There were about 10 or 12 steps below the clouds. There were more, but the clouds were covering them. I was so surprised that I reached out to my wife and grabbed her arm and shouted. "Do you see the stairs?" Just then, a voice said, "Come on up"!

*"Come on up"!*

I woke my wife up and grabbed her. She then woke up, and we were so excited that God was inviting us to Heaven. That is when I realized that God is inviting all of us to "come on up".

***Welcome to the Kingdom of Heaven!***

# Appendices

### Top Ten Historical References to Jesus Outside of the Bible

https://biblearchaeologyreport.com/2022/11/18/top-ten-historical-references-to-jesus-outside-of-the-bible/

### Evidence from Tacitus

https://www.bethinking.org/jesus/ancient-evidence-for-jesus-from-non-christian-sources

### Non-canonical books referenced in the Bible

https://en.wikipedia.org/wiki/Non-canonical_books_referenced_in_the_Bible

### Is There Any Evidence For Jesus Outside The Bible?

https://coldcasechristianity.com/writings/is-there-any-evidence-for-jesus-outside-the-bible/

### The Bible Says Jesus Was Real. What Other Proof Exists?

https://www.history.com/news/was-jesus-real-historical-evidence

### Jesus Outside the Bible, 1 – Tacitus

https://reasonabletheology.org/jesus-outside-the-bible-1-tacitus/

www.ingramcontent.com/pod-product-compliance
Lightning Source LLC
Chambersburg PA
CBHW070542010526
44118CB00012B/1194